The Process of Faith

From God's Hands to Yours

By Nathaniel R Horton

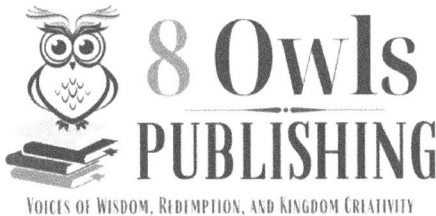

8 Owls
PUBLISHING
VOICES OF WISDOM, REDEMPTION, AND KINGDOM CREATIVITY

The Process of Faith

8 Owls Publishing creates books that effectively advance God's Kingdom. You may find the full list of the books we offer on our website at 8owlspublishing.com.

First Edition

Please note that 8 Owls Publishing uses capitalization when referencing God and/or other Kingdom terminology that may differ from other publishers or grammatical trends. 8 Owls Publishing uses the English Standard Version of the Bible, published by Crossway in Wheaton, Illinois, unless otherwise noted.

ESV: Study Bible: English Standard Version. Wheaton, Ill: Crossway Bibles, 2007. Print.

ISBN: 978-1-952618-13-0

Forward

Over 4 years ago I walked into a small church just south of the DFW metroplex and met a young man named Nathan Horton. I hadn't seen anyone preach with such passion in a long time and was mesmerized at the way he handled the Word but was also moved by the Spirit. I could tell his heart had been captivated by the cross. It's easy to be passionate and bold when you're in love with the One you are talking about. This book has not been birthed out of a momentary revelation or a contemporary concept; it has been birthed out of his everyday life in scripture and a Spirit led understanding of the finished work.

This book is a clarion call to the simplicity of grace and faith and how beautifully they portray the Father Himself. As an evangelist I have the glorious task of revealing this every day to people and watch as their lives are transformed. Nathan does an incredible job of explaining the step-by-step process of faith and how it works hand in hand with grace. For example the second chapter of Ephesians says we go from being …. "dead in our trespasses and sin" to now "in Christ Jesus you who once were far off have been brought near by the blood of Christ." This is scandalous and beautiful all at the same time. The simple truth is just that…… simple!

I'll warn you now, when you read this book, your life….and hopefully the lives of those around you will change! You might just return back to the joy, passion, and zeal you once knew when you encountered the God of the Bible. Now buckle up and get ready as Nathan takes you on a life changing journey into the burning heart of God.

Evangelist Russell Wood; Founder and Director of Firebase DFW

Table of Contents

Introduction

Enemy of Our Belief
Enemy of Our Hope
Enemy of Our Faith
Enemy of Prayer
Conclusion

Introduction
  In the Beginning
  The Truth About Humanity
  Separation
  Heartbroken
  Grace Trap
  Summarizing

Introduction
  Lack of Faith
  Nature of Faith
  Conclusion

INTRODUCTION

The concepts of grace and faith have been pivotal in my life. The approach God took with me in my theological development ensured that I didn't receive my entire belief system from a single denomination. This created a desire for balance in biblical understanding. Balance is key; and balance is the heartbeat behind this book. My biblical roots began in the faith movement. God then led me in, out, and through understanding grace, often going back and forth between the two concepts. Because of this, I have a desire for the full picture of how they are interrelated. Over the years, I have listened from afar to ministers who have a balanced view in combining grace and faith. This has influenced my perceptions and simultaneously helped to formulate a game plan in which to teach and explain a more balanced approach.

I have heard many messages and teachings on faith and grace separately but have rarely heard an emphasis on how they work together in revealing the manifestation of God's goodness in our lives. To clarify, grace is God's part, while faith is ours. I have heard it said that grace is God holding our hand, while faith is us holding His. They work in tandem, depending on each other, thriving together, and yet the discussion is rare as it pertains to how their relationship is carried out.

If we focus on one aspect while leaving out the other, our understanding is unbalanced, and the practice of that understanding is unfruitful. This may birth doubt and hesitancy, leading to abandonment of vital concepts. Grace without faith can produce laziness and a lack of mobility in leaving it all to God. While faith without grace lends itself to legalism, highlighting our own efforts at the cost of His. When both are brought to the forefront as partners, true companionship with Christ begins. This allows fruit to be produced and Christ's heart can be brought forth into the earth.

In this book, I highlight the importance of partnership with God and what that looks like in the many different eras of the Bible. We will discuss what it truly means to partner with God and what He has done to set the stage for that to be possible. We will see how God has established the concept of covenant as the foundation and the birthing station of His partnership with us. And we will witness the role that God chosen to fill within our lives, as well as our position in Christ, as we labor with Him to bring His will to manifestation.

The purpose of this book isn't to convince you of one way or another; it's not my purpose to convince anyone. My role in this matter is to portray what I believe the Holy Spirit has revealed to me. I leave it up to you to determine if what is discussed is appropriate for you. A child must be fed, but a mature adult determines what is considered nutritious.

It is my heart's desire that those who read this book, gain fresh insight into how the pillar concepts discussed in this book are used in our Christian walk-and how they relate and cooperate with one another. My goal is to get you thinking, and through the leading of the Holy Spirit, venture into a journey you might not have deemed possible. I pray that a new level of partnership with God is birthed within you through what is expressed on these pages. May this spark a renewal in your walk with God, deepen your relationship with Him, and increase your resolve in receiving from Him. God knows how to partner with us, so let's learn how to partner with Him.

Chapter 1: Foundational Overview

IT'S A PROCESS, NOT A FORMULA

First things first, the title of this book is not by accident for I wish to convey a foundational perception about the steps needed. First, faith isn't a formula. It's a process. It's not something that is memorized, copied, and applied in which you get the same output if you continue to insert the same input. It's not a system of rules that if followed will produce the same exact results no matter the situation. It's not mathematical in its approach but is founded and based in a relationship.

> *"Looking unto Jesus the author and finisher of our faith; ..."*
> **Hebrews 12:2 (KJV)**

An author is responsible for how the story is played out. They set the tone of the narrative and establish key points in the development of the work. This is true of Jesus in the carrying out of our faith. He doesn't just give us a list of things to do in order to get specific results. That doesn't result in true family connection. Jesus is highly relational. Faith isn't about doing this to get that, but rather listening to the Man who did all that was needed for us to have abundant life through faith.

In **Jeremiah 5:1 (KJV)**, God said to the prophet Jeremiah, **«Before I formed thee in the belly I knew thee; and before thou camest forth out of the womb I sanctified thee, and I ordained thee a prophet unto the nations.»** The key point I want to highlight is the fact that Jeremiah was formed in the womb and even before he was created, he was known. God's knowledge of Jeremiah is what led to how God created Jeremiah. It's the same with us. His knowledge of us before we even made a choice is what greatly influenced our creation. If our origin was influenced by His knowledge of us, then why would our Christian walk be any different? If our very entrance into this world was by His intimate awareness of us, then how we live this life must be influenced by the same. How are we to live this life? Let's look to the following scriptures:

"For therein is the righteousness of God revealed from faith to faith: as it is written, 'The just shall live by faith.'" **Romans 1:17 (KJV)**

"But that no man is justified by the law in the sight of God, it is evident: for, 'The just shall live by faith.'" **Galatians 3:11 (KJV)**

"Now the just shall live by faith…" **Hebrews 10:38 (KJV)**

It is made clear, that the just or the justified, those who have been declared righteous, are to live by faith. The very life we were created into, we are to live by faith. That being the very faith that Jesus is writing for us every day. Just like my personal story is nothing like anyone else's, likewise, my faith story with my Author is incomparable. He deals with me differently than He might someone else, which in turn brings dependence upon Him

2

and His ways. The tasks He has me do for a desirable goal would not be the same path He would take with someone else.

I think this is where some people miss it in the beginning stages of their faith journey. They see someone do a specific task which creates a specific result that is very pleasing. The success story makes bystanders want to replicate the results- copy every form of the task.

But just because someone sowed a car into a ministry ending up with God blessing them with a better car, doesn't mean the task has become an equation. If you were to do the same without the leading of the Holy Spirit, you might be walking to work for a while. You don't know what God was doing through the obedience of that individual. Maybe cars had taken God's place in their life. Maybe it was a lesson in generosity, or preparation for greater blessing in the coming weeks. No matter the case, just because the process was successful doesn't mean we turn it into an equation. Giving your car won't get you another car unless God has willed to do so. Don't make the mistake of using someone else's form of sacrifice as your shortcut to the result. Jesus is not only the Author, but the Finisher. Trust Him in the process as you approach the conclusion.

THE BRIDGE

Let's look at the core of this selection-the relationship between grace and faith. When I first started moving towards a study in this vein, I was on a sabbatical. When I received the inspiration, I devoted a portion of my prayer time seeking guidance on how God saw the relationship between grace and faith. As I was praying, I saw a bridge develop before me, and instantly I knew that this was how God viewed the relationship.

I saw two cliffs with a huge drop between them. Stretching between the two cliff-sides, and over the drop, was a bridge. It was a metal bridge easily supported and framed by metallic beams. Going across the bridge from the left were many delivery trucks carrying multiple forms of products to the other side. It was then I realized how God saw the relationship between grace and faith. He sees them as a bridge enabling the transport of Heaven's goods into our natural lives. Let me give you a scripture:

"For by grace you have been saved through faith, and that not of yourselves, it is the gift of God; not as a result of works, so that no one may boast."
Ephesians 2:8-9 (NASB)

Here we see the origin of our salvation. We were saved (born-again) through grace. This did not happen through our own efforts. We could not pride ourselves on our own tactics and plans to make it happen, but rather, our salvation was a gift that came through the love of God manifesting in the form of Christh. **"For God so loved the world, that He gave His only begotten Son, that whoever believes in Him shall not perish, but have eternal life." (John 3:16, NASB)**. Notice that grace is what provided salvation, but it had to be channeled toward us. Salvation, and all it contains, was made available in Christ through grace. However all its components must be received by faith. Just because grace did the work doesn't mean we get to see the work. We must receive the work by faith.

If I were to give a gift to a friend, I would need to purchase it, prepare it, and then present it. But to receive it, the responsibility lies on the friend to reach out, lay hold of it, and bring it into their presence. It's not the role of the Giver to be the Receiver; just like it's not the role of the Receiver to be the Giver. Both parts must to be active for a successful transaction.

It's the same in matters pertaining to the Spirit. If there isn't a Giver, then there is nothing to be received, but if the gift is ready to be received, and there is no one to fill that role, then the gift will never be realized no matter the importance. This is the only reason why salvation hasn't manifested to all people-not everyone has stepped up to their place as Receivers. They have attempted to place themselves in the role of the Giver, a place that God has long held before we knew the position existed.

> *"First of all, then, I urge that entreaties and prayers, petitions, and thanksgivings, be made on behalf of all men, for kings and all who are in authority, so that we may lead a tranquil and quiet life in all godliness and dignity. This is good and acceptable in the sight of God our Savior, who desires all men to be saved and to come to the knowledge of the truth."*
> 1 Timothy 2:1-4 (NASB)

We can see from this scripture reference that God wants all people to be saved. And we know that He made it possible through what is presented in Ephesians and the gospel of John. If He wants all people to be saved, then why are some not? The answer is because they haven't received the gift of salvation. We gained access into the Kingdom because we heard, believed, and then received the gospel message. This is the process of how salvation is received, and since God's Kingdom was made accessible this way, we live in it according to the same manner. Grace makes it available, and faith receives what is presented. It comes as no surprise that to portray this idea, God showed me a bridge.

As I continued to pray, I then got a sense of where grace and faith were being represented in the picture. Grace was the left cliffside while faith was portrayed on the right. Trucks moving from left to right across the bridge confirmed even more the nature of the relationship between grace and faith. The side of grace was giving while the side of faith was receiving, thus the transaction of the goods within the trucks was being fulfilled.

The vision didn't stop there. Other concepts became more detailed and clearer. I had studied these concepts before and, on some level, knew their connections with grace and faith. I could see more pieces of the puzzle-more cogs in the alignment of the machine.

I then knew that I didn't need to simply focus on grace and/or faith but to bring into the mixture the other supporting concepts that the faith process must rely upon. Again, I have heard these topics taught, but never in a manner of how they relate and work together. How these biblical concepts work together in the support of the Process of Faith is a main focal point of this selection.

COVENANT?

As we move to the first step in the Process of Faith, I want to make sure there is a basic understanding of covenant. The reason for this is because, no matter what you read and choose to take in, if you practice it outside the mandate of the current covenant, the process won't bear any fruit, and a fruitless process will produce faithless action.

What is a covenant? A covenant is basically an agreement between God and His people. It is how He chooses to cooperate and connect to His people in that epoch or time. It is important to understand that God doesn't change. **"Jesus Christ is the same yesterday and today and forever." (Hebrews 13:8, NASB). "For I, the LORD, do not change; ..." (Malachi 3:6, NASB).** God never changes, but His covenants-how He works with His people-do. His nature and character are constant through the seasons and dispensations. Please note the difference between agreement and covenant. An agreement can be broken and sometimes nothing negative happens to the breaker. A covenant on the other hand, functions like an agreement, but it carries more weight. Those who break a blood covenant are usually put to death as a result. God's covenants are blood covenants.

Covenant is very important to God. He is the initiator and has established covenantal principles. It is His chosen method of interaction with whom He has relationship. Think of it as a legal contract laying out the steps and procedures of the agreement. If the agreement, contract, or covenant is maintained by all parties, the transactions, or blessings of the covenant, are transferred. To get a grasp of the concept, let's look at an example given in scripture.

"Now it came about when he had finished speaking to Saul, that the soul of Jonathan was knit to the soul of David, and Jonathan loved him as himself. Saul took him that day and did not let him return to his father's house. Then Jonathan made a covenant with David because he loved him as himself. Jonathan stripped himself of the robe that was on him and gave it to David, with his armor, including his sword and his bow and his belt."
1 Samuel 18:1-4 (NASB)

In 1 Samuel 18, we see Jonathan establishing a covenant with David. Let's highlight some key factors. First, notice the initiator behind the covenant. What caused Jonathan to make a covenant with David? Was it because he wanted what David had? Was he forced into doing it by some unknown source? If we look at verses 1 and 3, we can safely conclude it was out of love for David. What this tells us is that Biblical covenants are founded and established in love; and because their foundations are supported in love, they are carried out in love. Love is the heartbeat and the backbone of covenant. Without this critical component, every covenant established would be broken. The reason is found in verse 4. **"Jonathan stripped himself of the robe that was on him and gave it to David, with his armor, including his sword and his bow and his belt." (1 Samuel 18:4, NASB).**

When you establish covenant with someone, you receive all of who they are, taking it as your own. Simultaneously, you give everything that you are to them. It is a merging and a transference of life between the two representatives. That is why we see Jonathan removing his robe and armor, as well as weapons, and giving them to David. The robe was a symbol of position, and therefore, authority. The weapons and armor were a symbol of protection and warfare. By doing these things, Jonathan communicated to David that his position was now surrendered to David. If David went into battle, then all that Jonathan had control over goes to battle with him-Jonathan's resources are now David's resources.

If love wasn't the motivation behind this contract, this agreement could easily be broken. Love, by definition, seeks the benefit of others before self. Love **"does not act unbecomingly; it does not seek its own, is not provoked, does not take into account a wrong suffered, ..." (1 Corinthians 13:5, NASB)**. The moment David might act undeservingly, the love factor in Jonathan would ensure that his part remained active. To learn more about the intricacies of a Biblical covenant, I recommend Dr. Richard Booker's <u>The Miracle of the Scarlet Thread</u>. It's a fantastic read and provides context to how covenants work. This is pivotal to every New Covenant believer.

ABRAHAMIC COVENANT

Since the meaning of covenant has been established, let's look at the first main covenant of scripture and how it functioned. As we dissect it, see if you notice a correlation between the out workings of this covenant and the relationship between grace and faith. Seeing the grace and faith connection in this covenant makes it much easier to recognize the same within our current covenant. Understanding Abraham's covenant will help you appreciate and tighten your grasp on your own. Remember that the grace and faith relationship is based on two roles-one as the Giver and the other as the Receiver. Now let's see how this partnership is represented within the Abrahamic Covenant.

After the flood, God began His plan of redemption by raising up a nation that would birth the Messiah. Before there was a nation, there was a man named Abram. It is through Abram that this nation was formed. In Genesis chapter 12, Abram is called out of the land of the Chaldeans and told to go to a land that God would show him-promising to make him a great nation and a blessing to all the families of the earth. When Abram left, he took his nephew Lot. This is in disobedience to the will of God who wanted Abram to go alone. There came a point where the possessions of both Lot and Abram grew too great for them to live in the same area. They decided to separate with Lot choosing the valley of the Jordan, leaving Canaan to Abram. God made His promise to Abram after the separation.

"The LORD said to Abram, after Lot had separated from him, 'Now lift up your eyes and look from the place where you are, northward and southward and eastward and westward; for all the land which you see, I will give it to you and to your descendants forever. I will make your descendants as the dust of the earth, so that if anyone can number the dust of the earth, then your descendants can also be numbered. Arise, walk about the land through its length and breadth; for I will give it to you.' Then Abram moved his tent and came and dwelt by the oaks of Mamre, which are in Hebron, and there he built an altar to the Lord." **Genesis 13:14-18 (NASB)**

Notice what is being connected in this promise; the entire promise surrounds the land in which God is giving. Not only will Abram receive this land, but all his descendants. Notice that God has him walk the land and become acquainted with that which He is giving to him. Why is this important? Because this makes Abram fully aware of the enormity of the promise. Why would God give such a vast piece of land to one man? Truthfully, He didn't. He was about to give that measure of land to a nation. Do you see the vision behind this? The land was the anchor to the promise of "I will make you a great nation..." (Genesis 12:2, NASB). Do you have any idea how long it took for Abram to walk the land? I don't. But the time taken was filled with the pondering of how big his nation was going to become. The size of the land must equal the size of the promised nation. Now it only gets better.

> *"After these things the word of the LORD came to Abram in a vision, saying, 'Do not fear, Abram, I am a shield to you; Your reward shall be very great.' Abram said, 'O Lord GOD, what will You give me, since I am childless, and the heir of my house is Eliezer of Damascus?' And Abram said, 'Since You have given no offspring to me, one born in my house is my heir.' Then behold, the word of the LORD came to him, saying, 'This man will not be your heir; but one who will come forth from your own body, he shall be your heir.' And He took him outside and said, 'Now look toward the heavens, and count the stars, if you are able to count them.' And He said to him, 'So shall your descendants be.' Then he believed in the LORD; and he reckoned it to him as righteousness."*
> **Genesis 15:1-6 (NASB)**

Now remember what the promise focused upon-the land that was to be given to Abram and his descendants. It was this land that grounded Abram in the promise. We must understand that to Abram, the promise hinged on the land, but the land hinged on him having descendants, which at this point, wasn't looking likely. This is why Abram sparked the question in verse two. He understood that without an heir there wouldn't be descendants to inherit the land. The heir was the key to the whole thing. When Abram remedied the situation by a natural solution, God encouraged him to believe in an unnatural answer. Abram believed God when He told him that the heir he needed for the promise was to come from himself.

According to scripture, that belief was counted unto him for righteousness, or right standing with God.

"And He said to him, 'I am the LORD who brought you out of Ur of the Chaldeans, to give you this land to possess it.' He said, 'O Lord GOD, how may I know that I will possess it?" Genesis 15:7-8 (NASB)

"It came about when the sun had set, that it was very dark, and behold, there appeared a smoking oven and a flaming torch which passed between these pieces. On that day the Lord made a covenant with Abram, saying, "To your descendants I have given this land, From the river of Egypt as far as the great river, the river Euphrates: the Kenite and the Kenizzite and the Kadmonite and the Hittite and the Perizzite and the Rephaim and the Amorite and the Canaanite and the Girgashite and the Jebusite." Genesis 15:17-21 (NASB)

Notice the wording in God's statement to Abram in verse 7 of chapter 15. He says that God plans to give the land to Abram and his descendants to possess it. In other words, God was going to make it available, but it was going to be up to Abram and his descendants to take hold of the promise. Sound familiar? In verses 1-6, Abram is concerned about getting the promise. He knows that the promise is contingent on him having an heir and now that the heir is assured, he knows that the land, and therefore the promise, shall be accessible. In verses 7-21, the focus has shifted from the accessibility of the promise to its possession. He knows that the land will be given to him, but he doesn't know how to take it. That is what initiates the question in verse 8, **"O Lord GOD, how may I know that I will possess it?" (Genesis 15:8, NASB)**. What is God's answer? -He cuts covenant with him. The details of the covenant, as well as God's prophecy of Israel's Egyptian enslavement, is found in verses 9 through 21.

The point that must be understood is that for the land to be accessible, Abram had to believe that God was willing and able to do it. When it came to possessing the land, God's answer was covenant. In other words, God was saying, "We will do it together!" The cry of covenant is, "You are not alone in this! My resources are your resources, my ability is your ability." God was basically saying, through the entire conversation of chapter 15, not only was He going to give the land and therefore the promise to Abram, but through the legalities of covenant, He was going to partner with him to possess it.

GOD'S PART VS. ABRAHAM'S PART

Now remember that a covenant is a binding agreement between two parties, and the agreement stands if both parties meet the required criteria. This criterion is agreed upon by both representatives at the establishment of the contract. Each participant has a role. Does this sound familiar? -like grace and faith? When it comes to the Abrahamic Covenant, the covenant between God and Abraham, the representative of the future house of Israel, what were the roles each party fulfilled? What role did God perform and what was Israel supposed to do for the covenant to remain in effect? Remember, if the covenant isn't protected, partnership ends and therefore the possession of the promise can't be achieved. The specific roles are found in chapter 17.

"Now when Abram was ninety-nine years old, the Lord appeared to Abram and said to him, 'I am God Almighty; Walk before Me, and be blameless. I will establish My covenant between Me and you, And I will multiply you exceedingly.' Abram fell on his face, and God talked with him saying, 'As for Me, behold, My covenant is with you, And you will be the father of a multitude of nations. No longer shall your name be called Abram, But your name shall be Abraham; For I have made you the father of a multitude of nations. I will make you exceedingly fruitful; and I will make nations of you, and kings will come forth from you. I will establish My covenant between Me and you and your descendants after you throughout their generations for an everlasting covenant, to be God to you and to your descendants after you. I will give to you and to your descendants after you, the land of your sojourning's, all the land of Canaan, for an everlasting possession; and I will be their God.'

God said further to Abraham, 'Now as for you, you shall keep My covenant, you and your descendants after you throughout their generations. This is My covenant, which you shall keep, between Me and you and your descendants after you: every male among you shall be circumcised. And you shall be circumcised in the flesh of your foreskin, and it shall be the sign of the covenant between Me and you. And every male among you who is eight days old shall be circumcised throughout your generations, a servant who is born in the house or who is bought with money from any foreigner, who is not of your descendants. A servant who is born in your house or who is bought with your money shall surely be circumcised; thus shall My covenant be in your flesh for an everlasting covenant. But an uncircumcised male who is not circumcised in the flesh of his foreskin, that person shall be cut off from his people; he has broken My covenant.'" Genesis 17:1-14 (NASB)

The New American Standard Bible explains it in a way that I love. It uses key wording that indicates who God is speaking about when He refers to the roles of the covenant. If you look at the beginning of verse 4 it says, **"As for Me, ..."** **(Genesis 17:4, NASB)** as if to indicate that the following duties fall to God and God alone. By looking at the NASB version of this portion of scripture, you can count five different **"I will"** statements that God declares are His responsibility for His part in the covenant. These statements start in verse 6 and carry over to verse 8. God's duties for the covenant are as follows according to verses 6-8 of chapter 17:

1. God will make Abraham exceedingly fruitful. (verse 6)
2. God will make nations of Abraham and kings will come from him. (verse 6)
3. God will establish His covenant between Himself and Abraham and all his descendants throughout the generations. (verse 7)
4. God will give to Abraham and to his descendants for all generations the land of Canaan for an everlasting possession.
5. God will be their God.

Now these are God's responsibilities and therefore are out of Abraham and his descendant's jurisdiction. They are not responsible to ensure they are fruitful or whether the land is given to them. They are also not to hold God accountable for being their God. These are obligations that God will fulfill according to the legalities of the covenant. All Abraham and his descendants are to do, is to keep their end of the agreement and they can be assured, that God's part will be given.

So, the question is, what was Abraham and his descendant's role? By looking at the extensive list on God's end, surely Abraham's is just as big right? Abraham's part in the covenant is recorded in verse 10 which states, **"This is My covenant, which you shall keep, between Me and you and your descendants after you: every male among you shall be circumcised." (Genesis 17:10, NASB).** All they must do to ensure they remain fruitful and have nations and kings come from them, the land given to them forever, and God remaining with them forever is to be circumcised. That is it. God does all of that, and all Abraham, and everyone after him, must do to receive it, is to be circumcised.

You might be thinking that it doesn't seem quite balanced. I would agree with you, but considering Abraham's track record of lying, God couldn't lay the weight of the covenant on Abraham's shoulders if God wanted to ensure that Abraham was going to be blessed. Think about it, if Abraham, or any of his seed, had a pivotal role in the carrying out of the covenant, any discrepancy or mess up on their end would cancel the whole thing. It was God who would develop, protect, and prepare the nation for the arrival of Christ. God Himself took all the responsibility and weight of the agreement to ensure that the nation would be ready for the appointed time. Not to mention, God just loves His people too much to allow their possible mess ups to hinder Him from blessing them.

This is what we see in the Abrahamic Covenant-an agreement between God and Abraham stating all the benefits that God is authorized to present to Abraham and his seed for all generations. How do Abraham and his descendants receive it? -through circumcision. If they are circumcised, they keep the covenant, and they have free access to what God has made available through this covenant, including the promise. Did you notice the correlation between grace and faith in the covenant? How grace gives and faith receives what grace has given. It's the same theme in the Abrahamic Covenant. God gives, and all Abraham and his descendants must do to receive what is given is to obey God through circumcision. It's as simple as that. Now circumcision is an important topic and we will cover it more in depth in a later chapter.

To summarize, the Abrahamic Covenant was how God partnered with His people during that time. Everything they did was in submission to that agreement because that was how things got accomplished. Remember, the covenant speaks of partnership. If Abraham, and later Israel, remained true to the covenant, the promise was realized-not because of their efforts, but because of their partnership with their God. This was realized through receiving what He was giving. Therefore, understanding covenant is so important because it is how our partnership with God is defined during that dispensation. And here is the best part: the covenant in which we partner with God in today is **"a better covenant, which was established upon better promises." (Hebrews 8:6, KJV).** If you think Abraham and Israel had it good during that time, just wait until you see how we live today. We will have no choice in journeying through the depths of our own covenant as we step into the Process of Faith.

Chapter 2: Grace–the Giver

INTRODUCTION

Here we are, at the beginning of the Process of Faith. By this point, I hope you have a firm foundation built upon the environment in which this process thrives. This specific environment is made up of the covenant that is reigning during the time. You might not have a strong understanding of the New Covenant in which we live and operate within today. But rest assured, you'll gain understanding as we go through the process. Remember, covenant is how our partnership with God is defined. And the Process of Faith, the process in which we receive what God is giving, is how that partnership is carried out. Let's start!

DEFINITION

What is grace? Grace is the first step in the process. It has multiple definitions, but for the sake of this book, I will only focus on two key points. The first definition is unmerited favor.

Many theologians believe and agree that one of the leading definitions of grace is that it's God's unmerited favor towards His people. So, what is unmerited favor?

Favor, according to Webster's, is a kind or helpful act that you do for someone. It also means approval, support, popularity, or preference for one person, group, etc., over another. Unmerited, again according to Webster's, is to not adequately earn or deserve. So, in summary, grace is God's kind and helpful actions towards you. His approval of you. His personal preference of you above everyone else. What has just been revealed is basically a watered-down version of how God sees you. It is impossible on this side of glory to put into adequate words how God views us, but it is so comforting and life-altering.

Paul prayed this concerning the church in Ephesus, "... **that Christ may dwell in your hearts through faith; and that you, being rooted and grounded in love, may be able to comprehend with all the saints what is the breadth and length and height and depth, and to know the love of Christ which surpasses knowledge, that you may be filled up to all the fullness of God." (Ephesians 3:17-19, NASB).** His prayer is that we would grow in our understanding and awareness of God's love for us, which is critical to our daily Christian walk. But His love is so vast, we will never be able to grasp its full measure. He is just that deep and just that good.

No matter how good all of this is, it only gets better when we add the unmerited part. Simply put, as the recipients of His love and affection, we can't earn it or deserve it. Everything that God does for and through us is initiated by Him and only Him. He isn't looking for us to do a specific act or a specific deed to earn or meet the required standards of worthiness. It's solely based on His love for us-not our actions. Yes, our actions are pivotal because remember, He has a part and we have a part, but we are currently browsing His arena, not ours.

Now let's look at the other definition. Many theologians agree that grace is also the power of God operating in someone's life-enabling them to do what they couldn't do before the grace was given. In other words, I like to call it a power boost. It's God's ability working in us and through us that enables us to do what we could never think of doing without Him. I believe, that because of the grace of God upon our lives, Christians employees should be sought after the most. Christians should be the most organized, the most gifted, the most administrative, and the most beneficial employees, not because of who we are in ourselves, but because of **"who is at work in you, both to will and to work of His good pleasure," (Philippians 2:13, NASB).**

Now remember, even though this is a different definition, it's still the same word, so both definitions are simultaneously working together. God's favor, power, and ability are all given, not because we have earned them or deserved them, but because He desires for us to have them. It's as simple as that. They are love gifts with no strings attached. He is the originator of the gifts. He has fabricated them according to His specifications. All we must do, is learn how to receive them. We'll get to that later.

I know that I've hammered this home, but let's do it again. Notice that the definitions lean towards you, the recipient of His affections and His attention. What this entails is, that when we discuss grace, it's all about how God sees us, and therefore, how He cooperates and operates with us and for us. It's His viewpoint of you and what He does in connection to that perception. It's all about His approach to us and therefore its God's part in the process.

GRACE HAS BEEN GIVEN

I have characterized grace as a Giver since, when looking at scriptures that focus on grace, giving is always associated. Let's look at a few examples. Often throughout the epistles, Paul mentions the grace that was placed on his life to do that which he was called to do.

"But on the contrary, seeing that I had been entrusted with the gospel to the uncircumcised, just as Peter had been to the circumcised (for He who effectually worked for Peter in his apostleship to the circumcised effectually worked for me also to the Gentiles), and recognizing the grace that had been given to me, James and Cephas and John, who were reputed to be pillars, gave to me and Barnabas the right hand of fellowship, so that we might go to the Gentiles and they to the circumcised." **Galatians 2:7-9 (NASB)**

What Paul is saying here, is that grace was given to him to preach the gospel to the Gentiles just like grace was given to Peter to preach to the Jews. The previous stated definitions help us to understand what is being shown. Paul is explaining that the power of God was given to him to preach the gospel to the specific people group in which he was called. Also, since it's categorized as grace, he didn't have to earn or deserve it. He just needed to receive and cooperate with it.

Still, the point is made that grace was something given. There was a purpose for Paul's life, and grace was given to achieve that mandate. He couldn't do it on his own, which is the reason for grace in the first place. Everything we are to do in this life, both naturally and spiritually, we are unable to do through our own power. Grace is the answer, and it is given to achieve victory and success in every arena. Look at what God tells Paul when he is confronted with a "thorn in the flesh."

"Because of the surpassing greatness of the revelations, for this reason, to keep me from exalting myself, there was given me a thorn in the flesh, a

messenger of Satan to torment me- to keep me from exalting myself!
Concerning this I implored the Lord three times that it might leave me. And He
has said to me, 'My grace is sufficient for you, for power is perfected in
weakness.' Most gladly, therefore, I will rather boast about my weaknesses, so
that the power of Christ may dwell in me."
2 Corinthians 12:7-9 (NASB)

Before this portion of scripture, Paul explains how he received a vision and multiple revelations that might tempt him to feel exalted or superior. A messenger of satan was released to attack him to prevent the exaltation. In the King James Version of the Bible, these attacks were labeled as a "buffet." In the original language, the word "buffet" means to strike with the fist; or give one a blow with the fist. The Greek word used for "buffet" is seen throughout the New Testament five different times. It doesn't refer to just one hit, but rather multiple hits. So, when Paul talked about this messenger of Satan, he was referring to multiple attacks upon his life. These attacks were designed to prevent him from pursuing his God-given mandate.

I can only imagine, that as Paul was attacked again and again, that he would ask God to help him. He would get attacked again, multiple times, and then ask God for aid. This cycle would continue with Paul asking for assistance from God, but God replying that His grace was sufficient.

I believe we all have stories like this. Maybe we are constantly bombarded with events or situations that are wearing away at us. We cry out to God for assistance to what seems like no avail. We don't hear or see anything that lightens or resolves our situations. What God told Paul is the same thing He tells us, that His grace is sufficient. That His ability working in tandem with our ability is all that is required to achieve victory in all situations. Grace has been given for our success. This is not just for our benefit, but for His glory and good pleasure. Again, it's not about earning, but receiving.

WE HAVE RECEIVED

We could go on and on about how grace is something that is given. I could take you to scripture after scripture that supports that fact. Instead, let's look at how it is given. Grace is given so that we might be enabled to receive from God, and in that, cooperate with Him for His purposes. The question is how do we do that? How do we, as natural beings, partner with a spiritual gift? It's just like God to give us the answer. And of course, it's not found in an idea, but in a person-a living, breathing, and above all else, touchable person.

"And the Word became flesh, and dwelt among us, and we saw His glory, glory as of the only begotten from the Father, full of grace and truth. John testified about Him and cried out saying, 'This was He of whom I said, "He who comes after me has a higher rank than I, for He existed before me.'"' For of His fullness, we have all received, and grace upon grace. For the Law was given through Moses; grace and truth were realized through Jesus Christ."
John 1:14-17 (NASB)

Let's break this into segments. Verse 14 talks about how the Word became flesh and dwelt among us. When we tie this in with **John 1:1 (NASB)**, **"In the beginning was the Word, and the Word was with God, and the Word was God,"** and then with **John 1:4 (NASB)**, **"In Him was life, and the life was the Light of men,"** we can conclude that the Word being referred to is Christ. Let's add another verse to strengthen this idea, **"Jesus said to him, 'I am the way, and the truth, and the life; no one comes to the Father but through Me.'"** **(John 14:6, NASB)**. Notice the words that are shared among the verses. Jesus refers to Himself as being interchangeable with life; and in John, we see the Word being the possessor of life. The Word dwelt among us is synonymous with Jesus walking the earth. And since Christ is life and this life is the light of men, this again connects to Jesus' statement about Himself. This whole verse is referring to Christ which is further proven in verse 15 of chapter

21

1. This is not a huge revelation, but still needs to be proven for the coming moments.

Verse 16 mentions about **"His fullness we have all received, ..." (John 1:15, NASB)**. Please notice the wording, **"His fullness."** Who's fullness? -the fullness of Christ. When are we going to get the fullness of Christ? According to verse 15, we already have it. This is crucial to understanding grace, especially when we talk about cooperating with it. Why? Because it must be understood that when we received Christ, we received all that Christ encompasses. I didn't just receive Christ as the Lord of my life, I received Him as the replacement of my life.

"I am crucified with Christ: nevertheless, I live; yet not I, but Christ liveth in me: and the life which I now live in the flesh I live by the faith of the Son of God, who loved me, and gave himself for me." (Galatians 2:20, KJV). You know the saying that parents like to live through their children? Well in this case, our Brother is supposed to be living through us. **"For the love of Christ controls us, having concluded this, that one died for all, therefore all died; and He died for all, so that they who live might no longer live for themselves, but for Him who died and rose again on their behalf." (2 Corinthians 5:14-15, NASB).**

When I received Christ, I received all that Christ is. This is important, so be sure to catch this. I'm not working toward the fullness of Christ. I already have the fullness of Christ. It's mine, I already have it. How? -because His fullness is in His person and since His person is united with me, I have all that He possess, not in some measure, but in its entirety. **"Neither pray I for these alone, but for them also which shall believe on me through their word; That they all may be one; as thou, Father, art in me, and I in thee, that they also may be one in us: that the world may believe that thou hast sent me. "(John 17:20-21 KJV).** As Christ was one with the Father, so am I one with Him. You cannot separate Christ from God. Therefore, you cannot separate Christ from me. His realities are my realities. **"By this, love is perfected with us, so that we may have**

confidence in the day of judgment: because as He is, so also are we in the world.» (1John 4:17, NASB).

Here's the point. I am in Christ and Christ is in me, therefore, all that Christ is, I possess. I'm not going to possess Him, but I already have all of Him in my life now, whether I see it or not. Christ has been given and I receive all that He embodies. Let's now get to the core of the chapter by highlighting verse 17 of chapter 1.

HISTORICAL PREVIEW

"For the Law was given through Moses; grace and truth were realized through Jesus Christ." John 1:17 (NASB)

In the King James, the word «realized» is the same word «given» as in the first part of the verse. That means there are two major points being stressed-one being the Law, and the other Grace and Truth. One was given by Moses while the other was given by Christ. What was the Law? It was a set of procedures and commandments established by God on two tablets of stone and given to Moses for Israel's instruction after Israel's departure from Egypt. **«Now the LORD said to Moses, ‹Come up to Me on the mountain and remain there, and I will give you the stone tablets with the law and the commandment which I have written for their instruction.›» (Exodus 24:12 NASB).** When the Law is mentioned, it is also referring to the entirety of the covenant God made with Israel. Evidence of this is found when we tie together 2 Chronicles 6:11 and 2 Chronicles 5:10.

"There I have set the ark in which is the covenant of the LORD, which He made with the sons of Israel." 2 Chronicles 6:11 (NASB)

"There was nothing in the ark except the two tablets which Moses put there at Horeb, where the LORD made a covenant with the sons of Israel, when they came out of Egypt." 2 Chronicles 5:10 (NASB)

Often, when we use the term «Old Covenant,» we are referring to the Law, or the covenant God established with Israel after their exodus from Egypt. If the Old Covenant, the possessor of the Law, came through Moses, what came through Christ? -the New Covenant, the possessor of Grace and Truth.

Remember in the previous chapter when I explained how covenant defines our partnership with God? It is the covenant of the day that lays the groundwork of how the people of that day partner with God. We saw how that worked with Abraham through the Abrahamic Covenant. Now we will explore how this covenant worked as the nation grew, seeing the origin and revealed purpose.

After Abraham, came Isaac and Jacob; from Jacob came the twelve tribes of Israel. Through Joseph, one of Jacob's sons, God was able to move Israel to Egypt to protect them during a drought in the land of Canaan. The Abrahamic Covenant was in full swing, making the nation fruitful in every way all because they remained circumcised. They continued to grow both in number and possessions to such a degree, that the king of Egypt began to fear their growth. Picture this for a moment: the blessing of God was so evident on the nation that other nations feared them. What did Israel have to do to be worthy of this? -nothing; all they had to do was know how to partner with God through the covenant.

In response to the growth of the nation, Egypt placed Israel in bondage, making them slaves. Moses, an Israelite, through a series of circumstances, escapes Egypt, and receives a commission from God to deliver Israel from slavery. After a series of plagues and other miracles, Israel is delivered from Egypt, travels through a wilderness, and ends up on the plains of Mt. Sinai. That was a rough summary, but the whole story is found in the book of Exodus chapters 1 through 18. For our purposes, let's look at what God says to them now that they have been delivered from Egypt.

"Moses went up to God, and the LORD called to him from the mountain, saying, 'Thus you shall say to the house of Jacob and tell the sons of Israel: "You yourselves have seen what I did to the Egyptians, and how I bore you on eagles' wings, and brought you to Myself. Now then, if you will indeed obey My voice and keep My covenant, then you shall be My own possession among all the peoples, for all the earth is Mine; and you shall be to Me a kingdom of priests and a holy nation." These are the words that you shall speak to the sons of Israel.'" **Exodus 19:3-6 (NASB)**

THE PROPOSAL

Here's the situation: the children of Israel, led by God, through Moses, traveled from Egypt, through the wilderness, to Mount Sinai. Throughout the entire story, Moses announces to the people, as well as to Pharaoh, that they are to go to Sinai to worship God. That was the mandate of their exodus-their deliverance was to come back to worship, to be brought back to their God. They have been in Egypt for years, living within Egyptian customs. Now they were returning to their God.

As Moses approached God on the mountain, God told him what to reveal to the children of Israel. Be aware, this conversation is between God and Moses. Moses is to reveal the contents of God's message to the people.

God started His message off with a reminder of what He did for them in Egypt-how He miraculously delivered them from bondage and how He brought them unto Himself. This is a pattern with God. He starts His conversations with His achievements to influence your steps. Why? -because in covenant language, His victories become your victories. Near the latter part of verse 5, God listed His desires for His people. He shared with Moses that they shall be His own possession among all other peoples of the earth. They shall be a kingdom of priests and a holy nation unto Him. These are awesome words and an awesome moment for the people of Israel.

Here's the catch. Just like everything we have covered so far, God makes this available to this people, but they must take possession. I'm hoping this is becoming more apparent as we continue. How are they to do this? What is their role? God tells us in the beginning of verse 5, **"if you will indeed obey My voice and keep My covenant." (Exodus 19:5, NASB)**. If they obey God's voice and keep His covenant, then they will be His possession-a kingdom of priests.

Let's not just graze over this; the truth of the transition about to happen is within these verses. What did God say Israel was going to have to do? -obey His voice and keep His covenant. Let's approach these individually. Notice the wording of the first one; He says they are going to have to "obey His voice." Notice He didn't use the word commandments or commands. The use of the terms "commandments" and "commands" are normal to us, especially because we are familiar with the Law. But don't assume what He is saying because we know what is about to happen.

The phrase "obey My voice" speaks of an intimacy that "obey My commandments" doesn't carry. All that is required in obeying a command is knowing the wording of the command. Relationship isn't a requirement. God wants them to "obey His voice." In other words, He desires they listen to Him, know Him, and understand Him. The focus isn't the words that are being spoken, but the person doing the speaking. Words give action, but the person behind the words gives context. This screams of relationship. God wants them to live with Him and be with Him. He wants them to know Him as He knows them. And through this knowing, they shall become His possession and a kingdom of priests. He wants to reestablish the atmosphere and culture of the Garden of Eden.

Let's further seal this with the last part of Israel's role. Not only are they to obey God's voice, but they are to keep His covenant. Again, don't assume what this means because we know what is about to happen. Remember, the Law hasn't been given yet, so to what covenant is He referring? -the Abrahamic Covenant, the only covenant in place at that time. What must Abraham, and later the children of Israel, do to keep the covenant? They kept the covenant through circumcision.

Now here's the key to the whole covenant that hasn't been rooted out yet. Why did they circumcise themselves? We know they did it because it was required to keep the covenant, but there had to be an influence that caused their steps, a reason beyond just blind obedience. Let's go back to Genesis chapter 17.

Remember the purpose of the covenant was for possession of the land. To possess the land, there had to be an assurance that the land was going to be given. Before Abram could even entertain the idea of possession, he had to settle in His mind that God's promises were sure. To Abram, the land hinged on an heir, which God promised would come from Abram himself. Because God promised this, and Abram was familiar with God and His ways, Abram believed God and it was credited to him for righteousness. His belief is what settled the issue and what he believed was what had to be secure for possession to be pursued.

So why did Abraham circumcise himself, or to be more specific, why did God tell Abraham to circumcise himself? To answer this, let's look at Genesis 17:11.

"And you shall be circumcised in the flesh of your foreskin, and it shall be the sign of the covenant between Me and you."
Genesis 17:11 (NASB)

Notice the purpose of circumcision; it was to be a sign of the covenant. What is the purpose of a sign? To give direction, to direct you to a specific place. So, in this line of thinking, every time circumcision was performed, the act pointed the person to the covenant that God had established. It was an act to remind them of what God had done and the promise He made. You might say it like this: God had them circumcise themselves, so that they would always remember God's promises.

Abraham and the nation of Israel's role within the covenant was engineered by God to help them remember His covenant, His agreement and promise to them. Why is this necessary; because you can't partner with what you don't remember.

"Without becoming weak in faith, he contemplated his own body, now as good as dead since he was about a hundred years old, and the deadness of Sarah's womb; yet, with respect to the promise of God, He did not waver in unbelief but grew strong in faith, giving glory to God, and being fully assured that what God had promised, He was also to perform. Therefore, it was also credited to him as righteousness." **Romans 4:19-22 (NASB)**

Why was Abraham convinced that God was going to be faithful to His promise? -because of circumcision. Every time he saw the scar, he was reminded of the covenant God made with him-how God promised to make Abraham the father of many nations and that it couldn't be brought about through Abram's efforts alone. If you recall, when God made the promise to Abraham, He also made it abundantly clear that He would do it. The more he saw the scar, the more Abram came to believe what God said to be true. Abraham's single act of obedience was used by God to bring Abraham into a posture of belief that anchored Him in the faithfulness of God. Nothing could sway Abraham from believing God because the scar testified of the promises of God through covenant. Repetition brings conviction and conviction anchors you.

That is the secret and lifeblood of the Abrahamic Covenant-believing that God is faithful, that He is able to do that which He promised and allowing this belief to move you into a corresponding action of partnership. What was that corresponding action that Abraham did because of his belief in God?

"...yet, with respect to the promise of God, he did not waver in unbelief but grew strong in faith, giving glory to God..." **Romans 4:20 (NASB)**

Because of his belief in the faithfulness of God, established through the constant reminder of circumcision, when faced with a situation that would bring doubt to that promise, Abraham did not waver. Not only that, but he gave glory to God. He praised God! Abraham was so convinced that the birth of his child was a done deal, he praised his God for His faithfulness even though he was staring at impossibility. His belief moved him into action.

To put it simply, the Abrahamic Covenant is a covenant of grace that is received through faith. If you know anything about our covenant, then this should sound familiar. Why, because the New Covenant is very similar to the Abrahamic Covenant. In fact, it was built upon the same foundation. This is what God wanted to establish at Mount Sinai. He wanted the Israelites to believe Him and enter into a relationship that would produce a partnership like no other. For that purpose, let's look at their response.

THE RESPONSE

"So, Moses came and called the elders of the people, and set before them all these words which the LORD had commanded him. All the people answered together and said, 'All that the LORD has spoken we will do!' And Moses brought back the words of the people to the LORD. The LORD said to Moses, 'Behold, I will come to you in a thick cloud, so that the people may hear when I speak with you and may also believe in you forever.' Then Moses told the words of the people to the LORD. The LORD also said to Moses, 'Go to the people and consecrate them today and tomorrow and let them wash their

garments and let them be ready for the third day, for on the third day the LORD
will come down on Mount Sinai in the sight of all the people.'"
Exodus 19:7-13 (NASB)

The next question is this, "What did the people say about God's proposal?" Verse 8 gives us their response, **"All that the Lord has spoken we will do!" (Exodus 19:8, NASB)**. My understanding is somewhat radical. The Hebrew word found in the phrase **"we will do"** is the word 'asah. According to the Blue Letter Bible, 'asah is used for the words made, yielding, and make. These words are all found in the story of creation in Genesis 1 and 2. The first time this specific Hebrew word is used in scripture shows how God made the world. This word is unique in the fact that it portrays God's activity **"in the beginning."** Now of course it's used throughout the Old Testament, but the first time it is used outside of God's creative activities is in Genesis 3:7, **"And the eyes of them both were opened, and they knew that they were naked; and they sewed fig leaves together and made themselves aprons." (Genesis 3:7, KJV).** The phrase **"made themselves"** is the word 'asah in Hebrew.

It is very interesting to me, that the Hebrew word used to describe humanity's first action without God's help, is the same word used to describe Israel's answer to God's proposal of partnership. As if to say, "We will do it without you." Maybe what I'm saying is a bit radical, but let's look at what God says after He hears Israel's answer. He tells Moses to relay to the people that they need to consecrate themselves and He will appear to them in three days. He had them make boundaries around the mountain, warning the people not to come up or they would surely be put to death. Is it just me, or does this sound a little different than the God who was desiring a relationship earlier?

Notice what God says in verse 9, **"The LORD said to Moses, 'Behold, I will come to you in a thick cloud, so that the people may hear when I speak with you and may also believe in you forever.'" (Exodus 19:9, NASB).** What was the key to the Abrahamic Covenant?

-belief in God. So, why is it so important for God to make sure they believe in Moses if He wants them to keep the mandates of the Abrahamic Covenant? When reading through this part without paying much attention (like I usually do), it's easy to miss the subtle change that had transpired-the covenant has changed.

Israel's declaration of their ability to do what God wanted on their own, was in direct opposition to the Abrahamic Covenant. God's only response was a covenant change. God had them consecrate themselves and set boundaries around the mountain for them not to cross. Therefore, He wanted them to believe Moses over Himself. Moses would now be their messenger instead of the people speaking to God directly. God wanted to help them, but Israel wanted to do it on their own. God wanted a relationship, but Israel wanted rules. God wanted grace, but Israel wanted the Law. These events sparked the arrival of the Old Covenant, a covenant that operated through the self-effort of those who followed it.

Let me put it another way. The Gospel of Christ is this: I can't do it on my own. I need a Savior. I need help. Does that sound anything like Israel at this point? God had to get them to this place so that when Christ showed up, they would receive Him and usher in His Kingdom. How do you get a people to understand they need help? You give them rules to follow that they can't keep, and in the attempt, they will realize they can't do it on their own. This my friends, is the purpose of the Old Covenant and the Ten Commandments, to bring a nation to the end of themselves so they could allow God to step in and bring them into their full potential.

This is what is meant by the Spirit of grace: I can't do it, but I know who can. "**For the Law was given through Moses; grace and truth were realized through Jesus Christ.**" (**John 1:17, NASB**). It would be easy to jump into the New Covenant from here, but

let's continue in this vein so that we might fully see the inner workings of the Old. Here's the point I want to make at the conclusion of this chapter. The Law came through Moses, but grace came through Christ. Christ is the possessor of grace, so if you have Christ, you have grace. And if you have grace, you have all the help needed to be successful in every endeavor. Take the time to go through the New Testament and see all the help that Christ gives. He is our ultimate Helper. He is the grace of God working in us and through us for His good purpose. How do we partner with grace? -by partnering with Christ. He did what we couldn't do, so we can now do what we couldn't possibly imagine. The grace we experience in Christ is the ultimate game changer. Why would someone not want to cooperate with Him? Sadly, we refuse His help more often than we think and in the coming chapter we will look at Christ more closely as we continue talking about grace.

Chapter 3: Grace—the Person

INTRODUCTION

During the last chapter, we explored the first step in the Process of Faith. We showed how the defining characteristic of grace is the fact that it's something given. We saw how grace is given to enable those who are willing to receive it, to be successful in all they encounter, both in difficult moments and in carrying out the plan God has for us. Not only is grace given, but we learned that grace has been given through Christ. Our unity with Christ is a unity with grace. Everything He is, is now in our possession, including the undeserving ability of God. We don't have to wait on it, but already believe that we have it in Christ.

We also ventured into the origins of the Old Covenant, learning the purpose behind the Law. We saw how the Israelites wanted to do all that God instructed on their own terms, thus ushering in a different covenant. We saw how the Old Covenant began, now let's see how the Old Covenant operated.

WHOSE FIRST?

Now for every covenant established there is an agreement of policy. For the Abrahamic Covenant, the policy is recorded in Genesis chapter 17 where the specific roles are lined out. God's part was to be the Giver of the land, and this land would be given to Abraham and all his descendants. In that, God would make them fruitful, and the list goes on. All Abraham, and those who followed, had to do to receive all that God was doing was to become circumcised. Each had their role, and if both roles were fulfilled, the transaction was valid.

The Old Covenant's agreement of policy is found in Deuteronomy chapter 28. If we take it slow, we will see a key theme throughout this chapter that highlights the lifeblood of the covenant.

"Now it shall be, if you diligently obey the LORD your God, being careful to do all His commandments which I command you today, the LORD your God will set you high above all the nations of the earth. All these blessings will come upon you and overtake you if you obey the LORD you God..."
Deuteronomy 28:1-2 (NASB)

If we look closely, this contains key words deserving of our attention in comparison to the Abrahamic Covenant found in Genesis 17. Whose role was mentioned first in the Abrahamic Covenant? -God's role. Why? Because under the Abrahamic Covenant, God was the Giver, or the Initiator. He was the beginning of the process-the Initiator of the partnership that was to take place. Abraham and his descendants took the role of the receivers or the partners. That is why their roles came last. As receivers, their job didn't come into play until there was something to get. The Giver had to come before the receiver. God had to come before Abraham.

Again, this is key. Grace must come first. Grace is the Initiator of the partnership. Grace is God's part, and it is always God's part that begins the process. Remember this as we dig into the workings of the Old Covenant. Now, whose part was mentioned first in Deuteronomy chapter 28? **"Now it shall be, if you diligently obey the LORD your God, being careful to do all His commandments which I command you today, the LORD your God will set you high above all the nations of the earth." (Deuteronomy 28:1, NASB).** Whose role is mentioned first? Look at the fifth and sixth word of the verse. **"IF YOU"** are the chosen words to initiate the process in this covenant. In other words, it's the Israelite's actions that come first. Under the Old Covenant, it's the people's actions that are at the forefront.

Notice the process here. God said that if they follow all His commandments, the key phrase being all of them, then they would find blessing. The blessing came after their actions. They must do something in order for God to move on their behalf. Maybe you think that this is how we serve God today. If that is the case, then you have mixed this covenant with a **"better covenant, which has been enacted on better promises." (Hebrews 8:6, NASB).** You have taken the inferior in replacement of the superior. If you mix any policy of another agreement with a replacing one, you nullify both. It's that simple.

In direct contrast to the workings of the Abrahamic Covenant, the Old Covenant required acts of obedience before God would keep His part. This might secure any doubts to what was discussed in chapter two about how the Old Covenant began. If you remember, God wanted to start the process and make Israel partners, but Israel wanted to do the whole thing on their own. "God, you say what needs to be done and we will do it on our own." Once that was said, it changed the covenant. Basically, God's response was, "You want to do the whole thing by yourself-fine. For me to get involved, you must do something first. My blessing will hinge on your perfection." If they followed the Law in its entirety, then they were blessed.

The blessings they received if they followed the whole law is recorded in Deuteronomy 28:3-13. And boy it's a great list. The problem was that if they missed one tenet of the law, the contract was voided, and they received none of the blessings. **"For whoever keeps the whole law and yet stumbles in one point, he has become guilty of all." (James 2:10, NASB)**

It's also important to note what would happen if they disobeyed the Law. It was more than simply not receive the blessings. They would receive curses instead. To put it simply, the curses actualized the direct opposite of the blessings, with the bonus of intensifying. All the curses of disobedience are found in Deuteronomy 28:15-45. God is good and it grieved His heart to see His people incur the results of disobedience. But because of their hardness of heart, His blessings couldn't flow. His people couldn't experience what God wanted for them. So, to help in this, God established the sacrificial system. By doing so, they had a way to deal with the consequences of the curses and allow for the release of the blessings.

The curses greatly outweighed the blessings. Why would this be the case? In my opinion, it's because God knew that a day was coming, when a Man (Jesus) would do for them (and us) that which they could not do on their own. He would keep that which the Israelites, and humanity as a whole, could not keep (the Law). He would be successful where we tend to fail. His goodness would replace our fallenness. He would take on broken humanity, so we could become like Him. On that day, the curses would be removed. **"Christ redeemed us from the curse of the Law, having become a curse for us for it is written, 'Cursed is everyone who hangs on a tree'- in order that in Christ Jesus the blessing of Abraham might come to the Gentiles, so that we would receive the promise of the Spirit through faith." (Galatians 3:13-14,**

NASB). Because the curse is taken away, my only response in the presence of such liberation must be worship!

So let me tie this section together; the Process of Faith hinges on one crucial fact: that God is the beginning of the process. If He isn't the Giver, then we can't be the receiver. If He isn't active, then we can't be active. He starts it, and together with Him, we finish it. In the Old Covenant, this order changes. The people pushed God out of His place and took over, therefore putting God in their role. But herein lies the problem: The Greater can't receive from the lesser. We do not add benefit to His existence. God as the Creator can never receive from His creation to better Himself. It's His role as the Creator, who gave me life, to continue to give to me to maintain that life. It's my role as the creation, to partner with Him, so that my life will become what He has destined it to be.

It's always been about cooperation. If we go first, then He must empower what we do, but if it's not according to His design¯and trust me, we want it according to His design¯then He won't cause it to happen. If He goes first, it's already empowered and blessed and all we must do is partner and receive that which is successful already. It's time we step out of God's role and take up ours in the covenant.

APPROACHING THE LAW

Now at this point, I want to make something abundantly clear; there is a trap that the enemy can move us into when we talk about the Law. I know this because I fell into it myself. The Law was established because Israel wanted to do things on their own; to bring Israel to the end of themselves so that they might seek help from the One who loved them the most. With that being said, the Law was the most loving gesture God could display. Place yourself in His shoes. These were people whom

He loved. The ones with whom He wanted intimate relationship. When they refused Him, out of love, He gave the Law to bring them back to the truth that they needed Him.

The Law was God's perfect, righteous, and loving nature in written form. Everything He required wasn't just to give them rules to follow, but to protect them and to preserve them as a nation. Example: Why would you think He wanted them to worship Him and Him alone? -because worship seals your devotion and your devotion seals your future. God knew, whomever they worshiped would be authorized to direct them. God, being the loving God He is, wouldn't allow the enemy of our lives to be in the driver's seat. He required their devotion in order to be authorized to guide them.

I say all of that to say this, it's so easy to fall in love with grace, but sometimes we can have a callous approach to the Law. Grace is God, but the Law came from God. Grace makes me what the Law could not. Grace enables me to do and become what the Law required. The Law was holy, and grace makes me holy. The Law was righteous, and grace makes me righteous.

Grace has made me what the Law could only show me. I still have a part to play. Grace has made me righteous and holy, but I still must choose to partner with God to see those things materialize in my life.

The Law was the best course God could have taken. The Law was love in written form. All they could do was try to follow it. Christ is the embodiment of love. He helps us do what only He can do. We must learn to love the Law just like we love grace. They both come from God, and both point to the same person: Christ.

GOSPEL OF CHRIST

Let's look at the Process of Faith itself, at least its beginning. Grace is the first and it shall always be the first link in the chain. Grace is the Giver and therefore the Initiator of the process. Now if you remember in the previous chapter, Christ Himself is grace embodied. Let's make this more concrete. Let's go to the verse of verses concerning the giving of Christ.

"For God so loved the world, that he gave his only begotten Son, that whosoever believeth in him should not perish, but have everlasting life."
John 3:16 (KJV)

What is the defining characteristic of grace? -the fact that it is given, and by it being given, it is therefore, a Giver. Who was given in John 3:16? -Christ was given. Why was Christ given? -for those who would believe Him. God gave His life, so we could have eternal life. He gave so we could have. It really is that simple. Why did He give? -love. Love is the motivator of all that God does for humanity. Because love is His motivation, love is the influence behind grace. You can't have grace without love. Grace is always given, and love is the supreme Giver. You can't love and not give. **"I have been crucified with Christ; and it is no longer I who live, but Christ lives in me; and the life which I now live in the flesh I live by faith in the Son of God, who loved me and gave Himself up for me." (Galatians 2:20, NASB).**

The Father loved so He gave the Son. The Son loved, so He gave Himself. The Gift became the Giver. Again, that is the nature of grace. Grace was given and therefore it is empowered to give. Let's look at another verse connecting Christ and grace.

"I am amazed that you are so quickly deserting Him who called you by the grace of Christ, for a different gospel; which is really not another; only there are some who are disturbing you and want to distort the gospel of Christ. But even if we, or an angel from heaven, should preach to you a gospel contrary to

what we have preached to you, he is to be accursed! As we have said before, so I say again now, if any man is preaching to you a gospel contrary to what you received, he is to be accursed! For am I now seeking the favor of men, or of God? Or am I striving to please men? If I were still trying to please men, I would not be a bondservant of Christ. For I would have you know, brethren, that the gospel which was preached by me is not according to man. For I neither received it from man, nor was I taught it, but I received it through a revelation of Jesus Christ." **Galatians 3:6-12 (NASB)**

Paul criticizes the Galatian church for pursuing another gospel. How does Paul know that they are following another gospel, which in fact isn't a gospel at all? To get this, we need to first understand how we received this gospel. We received it through hearing, or for the sake of context, we were called to it, and we answered the call. Look at what Paul says in the book of Romans, **"For I am not ashamed of the gospel, for it is the power of God for salvation to everyone who believes, to the Jew first and also to the Greek." (Romans 1:16, NASB).** In order to believe, we must have heard. Heard what? -the call, and through our belief, we answered the call.

Now lean back into verse 6 of Galatians 3. Paul says that he was amazed that the church was deserting Him who called them. So, who was doing the calling? -God. It was God who called us back to Him, and we answered the call. How was He calling us? -by the grace of Christ according to verse 6. So, the grace of Christ, or the grace in Christ, or grace being Christ, no matter how you want to look at it, was responsible for calling us back to Him.

Remember that we previously defined grace as favor which also means a kind act. Compare that with Romans 2:4 where it says, **"Or do you think lightly of the riches of His kindness and tolerance and patience, not knowing that the kindness of God leads you to repentance." (Romans 2:4, NASB).** It is the grace of God, or the actions of Christ, that are the building blocks of the gospel message. According to Galatians 3, the Galatian church was deserting this Grace of Christ and turning toward a different gospel.

Here's the point: if they were deserting unto a different gospel, they must have been abandoning the true gospel. Look at verse 7, **"...which is really not another; only there are some who are disturbing you and want to distort the gospel of Christ." (Galatians 3:7, NASB)**. The gospel is and will always be the gospel of Christ. If it isn't about Christ, then it isn't the gospel.

What is the gospel specifically talking about when it describes Christ? -the grace of Christ. I hope it has become clear by now that grace and Christ are interconnected. The gospel is about Christ just like it's about grace. Grace and Christ are one. The main characteristics of grace are found in the person of Christ. So how do we cooperate with the grace of God? -by cooperating with the Son of God, the possessor of grace. When you submit to Christ, you submit to grace. It's just that simple. The gospel of Christ is the gospel of grace. Grace is motivated by love. Christ is motivated by love. Grace was given. Christ was given. Grace gives. Christ gives. Grace is the ability of God. Christ is the personification of that ability. He gives that ability a natural form.

It is so much easier to partner with a spiritual gift when that spiritual gift takes on physical form. Grace can talk to us. Grace can cry with us. Grace can lead us. Grace can touch us. Grace can minister with us. Grace can pray with us. Grace is with us always and will forever be with us to assist.

WHAT HAS HE DONE?

Now that we have established that grace is Jesus Christ our Savior, let's place Christ in His place in the Process of Faith. He belongs at the beginning. This is why I have spent so much time laying the foundation that grace is a Giver and therefore the Initiator of the process. To receive, there must be something to get. Therefore, the role of the Giver must precede the role of the receiver. Adding that to what we have just discussed, Christ is the beginning of the Process of Faith. He is the Initiator and the Giver of all that we could ever receive. All that I need or will ever require is found in Christ and because I am in Christ and Christ is in me, I am possessor of all that He is and has.

Here's my point at this juncture. Christ is the beginning of all things in the Christian walk. Therefore, everything I am and do, must begin with Him. If anything, I do or become doesn't originate in Christ, then it will not be fruitful. **"Abide in Me, and I in you. As the branch cannot bear fruit of itself unless it abides in the vine, so neither can you unless you abide in Me. I am the vine, you are the branches; he who abides in Me and I in him, he bears much fruit, for apart from Me you can do nothing." (John 15:4-5, NASB).** With that being said, I want to talk about seeing Christ as the head of everything and the Originator of all things I am to receive. He is the blueprint for my life. I can't do anything unless He has done it first or is doing it with me. Let's look at a very popular story as an example.

In Matthew chapter 14, there is a well-known story of how Peter walked on the water. If you've been in church for any length of time, you might have heard this story at least once. There is a key element that I want to draw out. The disciples are in a boat in the middle of a storm. Jesus walks out to them, upon the waves, and the disciples mistake Him as a ghost. Sensing their fear, Jesus says, **"Take courage, it is I; do not be afraid." (Matthew 14:27, NASB).** Here is where I want to camp for a moment:

"Peter said to Him, "Lord, if it is You, command me to come to You on the water. And He said, 'Come!' And Peter got out of the boat and walked on the water and came toward Jesus. But seeing the wind, he became frightened, and beginning to sink, he cried out, 'Lord, save me!' Immediately Jesus stretched

out His hand and took hold of him, and said to him, 'You of little faith, why did you doubt?'" Matthew 14:28-31 (NASB)

What was Jesus doing in this story? -He was walking on the water. This is not much of a revelation, I know. What was the thing that Peter wanted to do? -many would say to walk on the water. I would agree partially but look at Peter's statement in verse 28. **"Peter said to Him, 'Lord, if it is You, command me to come to You on the water.'" (Matthew 14:28, NASB).**

Peter wasn't simply wanting Jesus to ask him to come to Him. Peter wanted Jesus to command him to come. He didn't want Christ to request it of him. He wanted Christ to demand it of him. Why is this important? -because Peter understood that there is equipping within a command. If Jesus commanded Peter to walk on the water, then he would walk on the water. In this, Peter wasn't only walking on the water, he was walking on a command.

And where did Peter even get the idea of walking on the water? -from Christ Himself who was doing that very thing in front of him. We have no evidence to indicate that Peter contemplated the idea of doing such a thing without Christ doing it first.

The point is that Jesus was the Originator of the event in every fashion. Because Christ walked on the water, Peter received the idea himself. Because Christ commanded Peter to do it, Peter understood he could do it. The whole event was made possible, both in its conception and activation, because of Christ. He initiated this act of faith and gave the ability to fulfill it. This is the same principle in everything we do as Christians. He is the Originator of all our doings. We can't do anything unless He is either doing it Himself or has done it already.

What did Jesus say before He ascended? **"Truly, truly, I say to you, he who believes in Me, the works that I do, he will do also: and greater works than these he will do; because I go to the Father."**

43

(John 14:12, NASB). Notice the word "also." We do it because He has already done it. We heal the sick because He heals the sick. We deliver the bound because He delivered the bound. This is partnership at its finest. Because Jesus does these things, we get to do them also.

Remember, He is the beginning of the process. He is the Originator and the Initiator of all our endeavors. If He hasn't done it, or isn't currently doing it, then we have nothing to receive and partner with.

When sickness comes, what has He done? **"Who his own self bore our sins in his own body on the tree, that we, being dead to sins, should live unto righteousness: by whose strips ye were healed."** **(1Peter 2:24, KJV).** When poverty comes, what has He done? **"For you know the grace of our Lord Jesus Christ, that though He was rich, yet for your sake he became poor, so that you through His poverty might become rich." (2 Corinthians 8:9, NASB).** When bondage comes, what has He done? **"It was for freedom that Christ set us free; therefore, keep standing firm and do not be subject again to a yoke of slavery." (Galatians 5:1, NASB).** What He has done is a clear indication of what I'm partnering with Him to do.

We are discussing a process, not an equation. Let's say we find ourselves in spiritual warfare. What is the first step in the process of receiving from God, in partnering with God? -grace, or understanding that all that you need is already in Christ. He is the Possessor and the Originator of all that we could need. If it's something you need, you have it because He has it. He is in you, and you are in Him. If it's something you need to do, He has the ability and therefore so do you. How this looks to you will be different than how it looks to me. It's a process, not an equation. God deals with us differently, so the grace of God you see in Christ, will be different than what I see. However, it's still the grace of God and it's still Christ. Don't compare your partnership with someone else's. This is an intimate cooperation with Him.

COVENANT DEFINING

Let's get a little radical again. We have seen how Christ is the Originator and the Initiator of all our endeavors in this Christian walk. We can't do anything unless He has already done it. He is our blueprint and our example. Now remember, covenant is how we define our partnership with God, which includes our cooperation with Christ. We live in the New Covenant because it is the covenant that Christ brought us into. We will discuss that further in a later section. But here is the thing we need to grasp: Christ was a prophet under the Old Covenant. The New Covenant wasn't set in place until Acts 2 with Pentecost and the birth of the Church. The Old Covenant reigned supreme from Exodus 19 all the way up to Acts 2. This includes the Gospel of Matthew, Mark, Luke, John.

Even though Christ is our example, that doesn't mean everything He did on the earth we are to copy. He was still in submission to a covenant in which we no longer follow. It must be said that there are some things in the Gospels that Jesus did, that we are not to do. He did these things because the covenant of that time warranted Him to do so. But since we live under a different agreement, those things are not required of us.

This is why covenant understanding is so important. It defines our partnership with God. If we don't know how the Old Covenant operates, we will submit to an agreement that Jesus has already fulfilled. Let me give an example of this so you can keep an eye out when you read the Gospels for yourself.

Before I do, I need to say this: the Old Covenant and the Gospels are not to be thrown out as irrelevant. That is highly unbiblical. The Old Testament points me to Christ, while the New Testament roots me in Christ. The whole point is Christ and since Christ is the focus of the Old Covenant and the Gospels, why would I remove them? Both parts are necessary and are to be utilized, but in their respective roles. I look at the Old Covenant through New Covenant eyes. I see differently from where I stand in Christ. Let me put it to you this way-my New Covenant life influences my Old Covenant understanding. I refuse to allow my Old Covenant understanding to influence my New Covenant life. The New gives context to the Old, not the other way around. Now let's look at Christ in the Gospels.

Recall how the Old Covenant works-it moves through self-effort. It's all about how we don't need God's help to do what needs to be done. God simply needs to tell us what to do, and we will see that it is accomplished.

Here is a clear indicator of when the Old Covenant is popping up in a conversation within the Gospels. If someone asks the question of what they need to do, or what they should be doing, they are referring to self-effort. This is a clear indication of Old Covenant thinking. This is not bad, it's just the mindset of the day. Remember, the New Covenant hasn't come yet, so we can't expect them to think like New Covenant believers when they have lived under the the Old Covenant for so long. Some understood, others didn't. It's the same today.

Here is another tip to determine which covenant is being described in the Gospel conversations. When a dialogue with Christ is happening ask yourself these questions: To whom was Jesus speaking and what was the question? If Jesus was speaking to the Pharisees or the Sadducees, or any other religious ruler of that day, chances are He is using the Law. If Jesus was speaking with His disciples or a Gentile, such as a Roman or a Greek, these are clear indicators that He is using New Covenant language, especially if the person was a Gentile. Why? Because the Law wasn't given to the Gentiles, it was given to the Jews.

Remember the blind man who Jesus healed on the Sabbath? The man he healed was a Jew, but He didn't care that he was healed on the Sabbath or that the Law might have been broken. He was just overwhelmed in worship and thankfulness because He was healed. It was the religious leaders, who were well versed in the Law, who were trying to reason it away. The religious leaders told the healed man that Jesus was a sinner (a law breaker). They didn't believe it was possible for Him to heal in this manner since the power of God couldn't possibly move through someone who breaks the Law. After hearing this, the man said, **"Whether He is a sinner, I do not know; one thing I do know, that though I was blind, now I see." (John 9:25, NASB)**

If they knew the Law, Jesus communicated through the Law. If they knew nothing of the Law, then Jesus was able to go straight to grace. **"Wherefore the law was our schoolmaster to bring us unto Christ, that we might be justified by faith." (Galatians 3:24, KJV).** The purpose of the Law was to point to Christ and His ministry. The Law gave the Jews a picture of who to look for as the Messiah. The Law identified Jesus to the Jews so that when Jesus showed up, they could receive Him. Since the Law wasn't given to the Gentiles, Jesus identified Himself on His own. The Jews needed the Law to see Jesus. The Gentiles just needed Jesus. Now let's look at a Gospel conversation in which Jesus discusses the Old Covenant.

> *"But when the Pharisees heard that Jesus had silenced the Sadducees, they gathered themselves together. One of them, a lawyer, asked Him a question, testing Him, Teacher, which is the great commandment in the Law?"*
> Matthew 22:34-36 (NASB)

Let's ask our questions: With whom is Jesus speaking? -a Pharisee, a religious leader who happened to be a lawyer, someone who was well versed in the Law. What was the question asked? -the Pharisee asked Jesus about the greatest commandment in the Law. By looking at this information, we can conclude that this conversation was in Old Covenant territory. Let's see what Jesus said.

"And He said to him, 'You shall love the Lord your God with all your heart, and with all your soul, and with all your mind. This is the great and foremost commandment. The second is like it, 'You shall love your neighbor as yourself.' On these two commandments depend the whole Law and the Prophets."
Matthew 22:37-40 (NASB)

This one is easy to recognize, but often it is said that we as New Covenant believers are to do this. Jesus wasn't saying that as New Covenant believers we are to love God with all our heart, soul, mind, and strength. He was just answering a question that the religious leader had for him. So, Nathan, are you saying we aren't to love God with all our heart, soul, mind, and strength. I'm not saying you shouldn't. What I'm saying is that Jesus doesn't require it.

Let's unpack this further. Can you honestly say you love God with all your heart, mind, and strength? I'm not asking if you have a desire to, for we all do. What I'm asking is: do you now, at this moment, love Him with all your being? I can honestly say the answer for me is no. Now, for me to fulfill the law, I had to be able to meet that requirement, a requirement that is impossible for me to meet on my own. This is what Jesus was explaining to the New Covenant Church through this conversation. Under the Law, you were required to love Him. But now, He wants us to receive His love, enabling us to love Him.

Let me emphasize something here. I'm not overriding what Jesus said, I mean, He is Jesus! What we are doing is taking what He said and bringing it into the New Covenant. Remember, He was a prophet under the Law, and because of this, not everything He said was meant for New Covenant believers. We must look at what He did and said before His death through our viewpoint (which is after after His death). We have a different viewpoint than those with whom He conversed.

Do you realize how liberating this is? Do you know how many blessings the enemy has robbed from the Church because we try to love God in this manner so that we might earn and deserve what God has already placed within us in Christ? Again, you can't earn or deserve anything that God desires to impart to you. Just receive it because you already have it in Christ. You may be asking, "Nathan, if I'm not supposed to love God with all my heart, soul, mind, and strength, then how am I supposed to love God?" I'm glad you asked. Go with me to the book of 1 John.

"We love, because He first loved us." 1 John 4:19 NASB

Remember, Christ is our example. We can't do anything apart from Him. We can't do anything unless He has done it or is doing it, this includes love. God isn't requiring me to love. He is requiring me to be loved, and then allow that love to be brought forth. The love I give is the love that God has already given to me. Look at what Jesus says in the Gospel of John.

"A new commandment I give to you, that you love one another, even as I have loved you, that you also love one another. By this all men will know that you are My disciples, if you have love for one another."
John 13:34-35 (NASB)

I love this verse, because it is a perfect example of the separation of the covenants, and it is performed under the Old. First, the questions: To whom is Jesus speaking? -His disciples. What was the question? -Technically, there wasn't one, but the location of this dialogue helps us. They are performing the Lord's Supper or Communion. What is Communion? -a New Covenant opportunity for partnership with His sacrifice. And what does He say? -He wants them to love one another as He has loved them. In other words, how He loved is how they are to love. His love will become their love.

If you look closely, you can see this pattern: Jesus is our example and empowers us to live for Him. This is seen all throughout the Bible. Just remember, leave Old Covenant concepts in the Old Covenant, unless they have a New Covenant partner. We were required to love in the Old Covenant to be blessed. Today, under the New Covenant, we are loved, so we get to love. We are blessed to be a blessing.

Grace is the beginning of the Process of Faith. Grace is Christ, which makes Christ the beginning of all we can receive. He is the Originator and the Initiator of all we could ask, think, or even do. He gives, so we can give. He is, so we can become. He has, so we can possess. Remember this when you start to receive from God, settle it in your head immediately. Jesus is for you and never against you. He holds nothing back from your success. He has what is needed, and because you have Christ, you have it as well. This is not about you performing. It's all about what He has done.

Let's continue with the next step in the process.

Chapter 4: Belief–the Supporter

INTRODUCTION

Thus far, we have discussed the first part of the Process of Faith, grace. We have learned that grace has been given and therefore, a Giver. We see how Christ is the sole possessor of grace and a union with Christ is a union with grace. Christ, like grace, is the Originator and the Initiator of all things in our Christian walk. Everything we need or could ever need is found in Him. **"For in him we live, and move, and have our being." (Acts 17:28, KJV)**. He has given us all things, and because we are in Him and He is in us, we are possessors of all things.

We discovered that the motivation of Christ, and therefore grace, is love. Love for us is what has and always will move Him. Everything He does and will do is birthed out love. All in all, the message of grace is this: I needed Christ, Christ wanted me, and now we are together for all eternity. The main thing that must be accepted as we move to the next portion of this selection is this-grace is God's role. It's how He sees us and how He loves to work with us. Grace is God's part in the partnership. Now, we begin to see ours.

THE BRIDGE

If you remember in the first chapter, I shared a vision that is basically the portrait of this process. I saw a bridge stretched beyond two cliffs across a drop where I couldn't see the bottom. Moving across the bridge from the left to the right were delivery trucks carrying cargo. This represents the relationship between grace and faith-a Giver and receiver partnership. Grace was on the left as the Giver of the delivery trucks; faith was on the right as the Receiver of the cargo.

We understand that grace and faith are the main focal points of the picture since they are represented by the two cliff sides. They represent the core roles of the process, Giver and receiver, God's part, and ours. If you think about a natural bridge, the bridge stretches from one end to another. It serves as a connecter touching two points, in this case, cliff sides. But it's not the cliffs that hold the bridge up. They just provide direction for the cargo coming across and serve as points of contacts for the bridge.

What makes the bridge function are the support systems in place, such as the metal beams and nails that keep the bridge strong and stable. Likewise, when we talk about this bridge representing the Process of Faith, we must understand that there is a support system, much like the bridge, that ensures what comes across, gets across. This support system is called belief. The determining factor of that which is given being fully received is belief. Just like the bridge, what I believe also determines what can go across the bridge. Without belief, grace will give, but no one will be there to receive. Belief determines the receiver's viewpoint of the Giver and even their perceptions of themselves. This in turn could cause the bridge's success or collapse. Belief is critical to the productivity of the Process of Faith in how we partner with God.

DEFINITION

The word belief in scripture is often associated with the word faith, and rightfully so. They are so close together in definition and in practice that sometimes it's just easier to accept them as the same thing. The danger of accepting two separate words as the same, robs us of the understanding the Bible is obviously trying to convey by using different concepts. I will admit as we approach this, that in some translations, belief is translated as faith and vice versa, so it can get a little confusing.

What I have learned to do, is get a firm grasp on what each word means according to its individual characteristics, look at the context of the verse, and look up the word in a Biblical resource. The best way of Bible interpretation is context-let the Bible interpret the Bible. If context is supported, you won't go wrong.

The word belief, according to Webster's Dictionary, means an acceptance that something is true or that something exists. According to the Blue Letter Bible, the definition is: to think to be true, to be persuaded of, to credit, and place confidence in. By putting these key words together, we see that belief means to be fully persuaded of the existence of something, to place your confidence in it.

Now here's the thing to understand. When we talk about biblical belief, it is used as a verb. Belief is always active and requires action to be utilized. Often, when belief is used in scripture, action is attached to it. What this means, is that the defining characteristic of belief is that it should always move you to action. What you believe should move you or influence you to do something. If you don't do it, then you don't really believe it.

This goes very well with the above definition. If you are fully persuaded of the existence of something, then that understanding will influence you to cooperate with it in some manner. If you are not fully convinced of something's existence, then you will most likely ignore it. You can examine what someone believes by what they pay attention to, for if it has their attention, it has become real to them.

Here's an example. Most of you reading this book, are probably sitting in a chair. Why are you sitting in it? -Because you believe that it's going to hold you up. If you believed that it wasn't going to hold you up, then you wouldn't be sitting in it. What you believe determines your steps naturally and it rings true in matters of the Spirit as well.

What I believe will determine what I can or even what I choose to receive. What I believe will determine if I'm even able to partner with God to the full potential the covenant provides. Remember, covenant defines my partnership with God, but what I believe about covenant, determines the level of that partnership. The covenant sets the conditions, but what I believe determines how I navigate those conditions. Let's see how what you believe influences how you receive.

SPIRIT OF THE LAW

We started this process earlier, and we will begin to mesh some of the other parts of the process together. Let's see how some of these things associate with each other. It will become highly noticeable when we get to faith.

If you recall, at the beginning of the Old Covenant, we read of a group of people who wanted to do all that God required on their own, thus opening the door for the Law. "Now it

shall be, if you diligently obey the LORD your God, being careful to do all His commandments which I command you today, the LORD your god will set you high above all the nations of the earth. All these blessings will come upon you and overtake you if you obey the LORD your God." (Deuteronomy 28:1-2, NASB). God wanted them to understand their need of Him so He gave them the Law to bring them to the end of themselves. If they obeyed first, then they were blessed second. That was the role set up within the Old Covenant. You see this throughout the Old Testament, especially when they were captured by foreign nations. Their disobedience to the Law of God led to the curse being active in their midst. If they obeyed the Law, they were blessed.

Here's the point, the Law was holy. It was perfect in every way because it was created from a holy and perfect God. **"So then, the Law is holy, and the commandment is holy and righteous and good." (Romans 7:12, NASB).** The Law was a set of rules to follow to become that which God is, holy and perfect. Because of the fallen nature of humanity, it was impossible for the Israelites to be like God by following rules. The need to follow rules left the whole process to them and their effort, leaving God out of the picture. Without assistance from God, they were to realize through their repeated attempts to keep the Law, that no matter what they did or tried, they could never keep it in its entirety.

Sure, they might keep one tenet, but according to the book of James, if they broke one rule, they were guilty of the whole thing. **"For whoever keeps the whole law and yet stumbles in one point, he has become guilty of all. For He who said, 'Do not commit adultery,' also said, 'Do not commit murder.' Now if you do not commit adultery, but do commit murder, you have become a transgressor of the law." (James 2:10-11, NASB).** The whole point of the Law, was to bring the Jews to the end of themselves. They needed to realize their deep need of God and that He wanted them to live in His likeness. The Law, if viewed and cooperated with properly, was to train those who understood the truth that they couldn't keep the Law to please God. But One was coming who could. The Law was perfect, but it couldn't impart perfection. The Law was holy, but it couldn't impart holiness. The Law showed God, but it couldn't make them like God.

What are we talking about in this chapter? -that what you believe determines your actions. So, let's see this in accordance to receiving Christ. Matthew chapters 5 through 7 is what is referred to as the "Sermon on the Mount." I love the "Sermon on the Mount" because, at points within the sermon, Jesus so perfectly reveals how the rules of the Law were just the shell and not the real focus of how to live. Jesus is truth, and He reveals the truth of the Law during this message. Let's look at one of those principles.

> *"You have heard that it was said, 'You shall not commit adultery'; but I say to you that everyone who looks at a woman with lust for her has already committed adultery with her in his heart. If your right eye makes you stumble, tear it out and throw it from you; for it is better for you to lose one of the parts of your body, than for your whole body to be thrown into hell."*
> **Matthew 5:27-30 (NASB)**

In verse 27, Jesus quotes one of the Ten Commandments. He stated it word for word. A Jewish person would be familiar with this rule. Their belief about it was simple. They were not to do anything of a sexual nature with someone else that wasn't their spouse. This seems uncomplicated, right? Look at what Jesus said about this in verse 28.

Notice that He transcended their understanding from a physical act to the influence behind it. Ultimately, He said the Law does more than govern one externally. He explained that lusting after a woman reveals that the fallen nature is still influencing your actions. This is committing adultery with her in your heart, and that isn't living how God wants you to live.

56

Do you see how Christ has made keeping the Law much more difficult? He moved it beyond its natural meaning to the actual spiritual definition. If a Jew genuinely tried to keep the Law and noticed that they kept messing up, the only conclusion would be that there is something within their heart that hindered them from being successful.

That something is called the sin nature that was brought upon humanity due to what is known as the Fall in the Garden of Eden. This nature is why we have an overwhelming urge to sin. We can't help it because that is what we are prone to do-it is our nature. We are constantly leaning into sin and doing what God hates. This is what Christ highlights here. It's not the physical act of keeping the Law but the spiritual influences behind your actions that cause your success or failure. It's a hard-wiring of sorts.

The sad thing is that some of the Jews believed they were keeping it. But Jesus wanted them to understand, or believe, that no matter how successful they thought they were, they were miles behind where they should be. Look at a conversation Jesus had about the Sabbath.

"He entered again into a synagogue; and a man was there whose hand was withered. They were watching Him to see if He would heal him on the Sabbath, so that they might accuse Him. He said to the man with the withered hand, 'Get up and come forward!' And He said to them, 'Is it lawful to do good or to do harm on the Sabbath, to save a life or to kill?' But they kept silent. After looking around at them with anger, grieved at their harness of heart, He said to the man, 'Stretch out your hand.' And he stretched it out, and his hand was restored. The Pharisees went out and immediately began conspiring with the Herodians against Him, as to how they might destroy Him." Mark 3:1-6 (NASB)

Before we become critical of the Pharisees, let's look at their viewpoint. They only knew what was written in the Law. **"Remember the sabbath day, to keep it holy." (Exodus 20:8, NASB).** This was the core of their entire belief system. They were to keep it holy. In other words, the Sabbath was to be separated unto God. They were to do no work on that day, because according to Exodus 20 and Genesis 1, God rested on the seventh day and called it holy. Because God did no work, they were to do no work. By healing on the Sabbath, Jesus was doing work and therefore breaking the Law.

This is why the Pharisees were so frustrated with Jesus. He constantly challenged their understanding of the Law. Jesus wasn't breaking the Law. He was fulfilling it to the full measure of its meaning. The problem was that the meaning was so much greater than the Pharisees could see. All they could conclude was that Jesus was a Law breaker. Look at what Jesus said about the Sabbath before this encounter.

"Jesus said unto them, 'The Sabbath was made for man, and not man for the Sabbath. So, the Son of Man is Lord even of the Sabbath.'"
Mark 2:27-28 (NASB)

What was the Sabbath? -a day separated unto God. To do what? -rest. Because it was a commandment under the Law, the Jews were instructed to rest in order to be pleasing to God. Jesus understood their belief about the Sabbath, but He operated under its full meaning. What meaning was that? -this day of rest was made for the Israelites and their benefit.

Do you see what has happened here? Because of the nature of the Law, a love gift of rest and relaxation from a loving God had been changed to a live or die commandment for approval. Jesus operated from a place of knowing the Father's approval and love. He operated from the knowledge, "I am His Son." That is why Jesus could heal on the Sabbath without fear. He believed that His Father made that day for Him and His benefit.

Why would God do that? Think about it: God made a day dedicated for rest and relaxation so that you might gather your thoughts and get ready for the coming week. He doesn't want you stressed and overwhelmed. Did Jesus look stressed and overwhelmed? No, because He cooperated with God to benefit Himself and rest. To Jesus, the Sabbath was more than a day. It was a continual place of peace and rest in the love of His Father. His entire existence was the Sabbath. It wasn't a day that was separated unto God. His entire life was separated unto God. **"Therefore, I urge you, brethren, by the mercies of God, to present your bodies a living and holy sacrifice, acceptable to God, which is your spiritual service of worship." (Romans 12:1, NASB).**

Do you see how your belief system greatly determines what you receive? The Pharisees believed one thing and Jesus believed another. Because of what they believed, the Pharisees were greatly hindered in their application of life. Notice the focus of both the Pharisees and Christ-it was the Law. They both had separate beliefs and those belief systems caused different degrees of living. One was restrictive, and one was liberating. One was Law, and one was grace. One was Old Covenant, and one was New Covenant. This must be grasped when we are talking about partnering with God. What you believe about Him will determine how you receive from Him. What they believed about the Law determined how they received from the Law. It's the same with God and with us.

Also notice, that Christ was living New Covenant principles in complete submission to the Old Covenant. What this tells us, is that the life of a New Covenant believer is the fulfillment of the Old Covenant. What you do today in Christ and with His help, is what they were attempting to do in their own strength. Here's the best part. They tried to obey the physical command (don't commit adultery) and weren't successful. You get to do both the physical (don't commit adultery) and the spiritual (don't lust) command and become successful every time. Not because of you, but because of who is in you. GLORY TO GOD!

PERCEIVING CHRIST

We have looked at how the Pharisees and Christ differ in their beliefs concerning the Law and how those beliefs greatly impacted what they could receive, thus what they operated within. The Pharisees were one dimensional in this concept, due to the fact they were a people who looked at Jesus from a distance. Let's now look at someone who was up close and personal with Christ and still needed a belief correction. His name is Peter.

"Now when Jesus came into the district of Caesarea Philippi, He was asking His disciples, 'Who do people say that the Son of Man is?' And they said, 'some say John the Baptist; and others, Elijah: but still others, Jeremiah, or one of the prophets.' He said to them, 'But who do you say that I am?' Simon Peter answered, 'You are the Christ, the Son of the living God.' And Jesus said to him, 'Blessed are you, Simon Bar-Jonah, because flesh and blood did not reveal this to you, but My Father who is in heaven. I also say to you that you are Peter, and upon this rock I will build My church; and the gates of Hades will not overpower it. I will give you the keys of the kingdom of heaven; and whatever you bind on earth shall have been bound in heaven, and whatever you loose on earth shall have been loosed in heaven.'" Matthew 16:13-19 (NASB)

The question Jesus asked His disciples was basically this, "What do you believe?" Peter said he believed that Jesus was the Christ, the Anointed One. Jesus then congratulated Peter and told him that this information was revealed, not by man, but by God. Let's jump a few verses ahead to another Jesus-Peter conversation.

"From that time Jesus began to show His disciples that He must go to Jerusalem and suffer many things from the elders and chief priests and scribes, and be killed, and be raised up on the third day. Peter took Him aside and began to rebuke Him, saying, 'God forbid it, Lord! This shall never happen to You.' But He turned and said to Peter, 'Get behind Me, Satan! You are a stumbling block to Me; for you are not setting your mind on God's interests, but man's.'" Matthew 16:21-23 (NASB)

We have two instances here where Peter shared what he believed. In one occurrence, he is praised by Christ. In the other he is rebuked-and they are both in the same chapter of the scriptures. My question to you is this, «What changed?» What caused Peter to be right on the money at one moment then be completely off the mark in the next? The answer is found in verse 23 where it states, «**for you are not setting your mind on God's interests, but man's.» (Matthew 16:21-23, NASB).**

What we have here is a man who walked with Christ, ate with Christ, talked with Christ. He lived his entire life around one man-Christ. Because of this, when he was asked what he believed about this man, Peter boldly declared, «You are the Christ!» Jesus tells him, after this declaration of what he believed, that this was revealed to him by God, not man.

Here's the point: God told Peter the truth, through what he witnessed. He saw Jesus's ministry. He heard Jesus speak. He witnessed Jesus's life. With every expression Peter experienced, God highlighted parts of Jesus's actions and then tied them back to what knowledge Peter had of the Law. The Law gave context to what He witnessed confirming what he came to believe. So why was he correct in the first encounter? -Because the context came from God. What he believed was influenced by God's touch.

In the second encounter, Jesus told Peter that his mind was set on man's ways and not God's. He had allowed the revelation about Christ to become the purpose instead of a part of the process. Beliefs lead to other beliefs and what you believe determines what you receive. You can't believe one thing without first coming to terms with another. With each new revelation God shows you, He increases your capacity to receive and therefore perform. Each new step births excitement and passion that we don't want to lose. Sometimes when God shows the next step, from our viewpoint it looks like the destruction of all that we hold dear. However, God is simply building on what has already been established. Each fresh revelation we come to believe is just the next stepping-stone to the bigger picture that God is developing. It's all a process. Be careful in allowing a single climactic moment to become the whole story.

How is this connected to partnering with God? -Often what we believe can get in the way of what we are able to receive, and therefore perform. Peter allowed what he believed to become the whole picture. When that picture was challenged, he couldn't move beyond. Although we often do this ourselves, God is still God. Christ did with Peter what God does with us if we allow Him. He tells us where we are messing up. We then submit, and correction leads to the next step. Don't allow the enemy to take this truth and cause fear. God is for you and is with you until the end of all time. He knows when our beliefs are getting in the way. Just remain teachable and allow God to do the correcting.

BEGINNING AND OPERATION OF BELIEF

We have discussed how belief is the support system to how we partner with God or, the Process of Faith. What we believe will determine what can be done in that partnership. We have seen that how we believe about a matter greatly influences what we receive from that matter. We have seen that what we believe often leads us to other beliefs which is how God increases our capacity to do more with Him. Remember, if I believe it, I will do it.

However, you might be thinking, this is all great, but how do I believe something to begin with? If believing is so important, how do I begin the process to believe something? Glad you asked.

"...for 'Whoever will call on the Name of the Lord will be saved.' How then will they call on Him in whom they have not believed? How will they believe in Him whom they have not heard? And how will they hear without a preacher? How will they preach unless they are sent? Just as it is written, 'How beautiful are the feet of those who bring good news of good things!' However, they did not all heed the good news; for Isaiah says, 'Lord, who has believed our report?' So, faith comes from hearing, and hearing by the word of Christ."
Romans 10:13-17 (NASB)

This is the process of salvation-of being born again. If this is how you came into eternal life, then this is how you also live this life. Salvation came when you called on the "Name of the Lord." To call on Him, you needed to know about Him. To know about Him, you needed to hear about Him. The pivotal component to belief is hearing. What you consistently hear, is what you will come to believe. Look at what it says in verse 16; **"However, they did not all heed the good news; for Isaiah says, 'Lord, who has believed our report?'" (Romans 10:13-17, NASB).**

Remember, belief moves you into action. If you believe it, then you will do it. How did Paul know that people didn't receive the good news? Because they didn't do it-they didn't partner with it. This question of concern from Paul also bears another message. Apparently, Paul understood that the stage was set for them to believe. How did he know? -the good news had been preached.

If you can hear it, you can believe it. If you believe it, you can do it. If you do it, then you will see it. What I just said is one of the most foundational principals to the Process of Faith-to receiving from and partnering with God. When you hear Him, you can believe Him, which will lead you to working with Him, which will ultimately lead you to see what you're working with Him to accomplish. This is manifestation!

"But prove yourselves doers of the word, and not merely hearers who delude themselves. For if anyone is a hearer of the word and not a doer, he is like a man who looks at his natural face in a mirror; for once he has looked at himself

and gone away, he has immediately forgotten what kind of person he was. But one who looks intently at the perfect law, the law of liberty, and abides by it, not having become a forgetful hearer but an effectual doer, this man will be blessed in what he does." James 1:22-25 (NASB)

This is another favorite verse of mine. Notice the connection between believing and seeing. In verse 23, James tells us that if you don't do what you are hearing, then it's like leaving the mirror after you have looked into it. What happens when you leave the mirror? -You forget what you saw. Why is this bad? -Because what you see is what you become. What you forget has no influence for transformation. The doing of the word is how you see the word; and when you see the word, you become the word.

Therefore, people do not see change in their lives. They claim they believe that God heals, delivers, and provides, but when you ask what they are doing regarding their belief, they say, "Nothing." Because they are doing nothing, there is no natural link to what they are spiritually believing. If you believe it, you will do it. If you believe it, you will partner with it.

Let's talk about an easy example-provision. The easiest representation of provision is money. Let's say you need to pay a bill and you need more money to do so. Grace-the first part in the Process of Faith, the first part in receiving from and partnering with God-tells us that you have all that you need in Christ. He is the Giver. **"And this same God who takes care of me will supply all your needs from his glorious riches, which have been given to us in Christ Jesus." (Philippians 4:19, NLT).** I love the New Living Translation Version of this verse, because it plainly states we already have everything we need in Christ.

Moving forward in the process, now I've heard the truth. This is the report that God asks me to believe. Do I believe that all my needs are met because of the riches that have been given to me in Christ? If I believe it, then I will do it. How do I do it? How do I partner with God in it? -by giving!

Here is where people sometimes get confused. Remember, grace is the beginning. Grace is the influence behind what I do. What does grace say? -I already have it in Christ. If I already have it, then I'm not trying to get it. I'm not giving to get. I'm giving because I already have. You are not operating from a place of lack. You are operating from a place of abundance in Christ. This is the method of partnering with God. I believe I have everything needed in Christ, so I give out of that abundance to partner with God to bring forth what I believe I already possess.

"Will a man rob God? Yet you are robbing Me! But you say, 'How have we robbed you?' In tithes and offerings. You are cursed with a curse, for you are robbing Me, the whole nation of you! Bring the whole tithe into the storehouse, so that there may be food in My house, and test Me now in this," says the LORD of hosts, "if I will not open for you the windows of heaven and pour out for you a blessing until it overflows." **Malachi 3:8-10 (NASB)**

This is the main scripture used to teach on tithing, and it is Old Covenant. How can I rob God when, in Christ, I already have all that He has? How can I rob from myself? Notice what is happening because they didn't tithe-they were cursed. I don't live under a curse because Christ took my curse. Notice what they had to do to get blessed-they had to give. I'm already blessed because I'm in Christ. They were commanded to give then, but we get to give now, all because of what Christ has already given in Himself. This is what Paul says about giving under the New Covenant.

"Now this I say, he who sows sparingly will also reap sparingly, and he who sows bountifully will also reap bountifully. Each one must do just as he has purposed in his heart, not grudgingly or under compulsion, for God loves a cheerful giver. And God is able to make all grace abound to you, so that always

having all sufficiency in everything, you may have an abundance for every good deed." **2 Corinthians 9:6-8 (NASB)**

We can call verse 6 "the Law of Sowing and Reaping." This is not Old Covenant. This is a law of the earth and God established this in the beginning, during creation, before the Old Covenant. Do I believe that what I sow I shall reap? -Farmers knows this to be true. So yes, if I believe it, I will do it. "The Law of Sowing and Reaping" is a grace gift given to me from a loving Father, who desires partnership with Him in the area of productivity. This works with money, time, items of value, etc...

In verse 7 we see the New Covenant mindset behind our giving. We already have all that we need in Christ. So, when God says to give, we do not need to be resentful. We recognize the partnership in operation concerning our finances. We are cheerful, because we know that God is working with us for increase, and above all, the working of His good pleasure and the advancement of His Kingdom.

Verse 8 tells us what happens while we partner with God in the realm of our finances. Through partnership, grace flows, making us sufficient in every endeavor. We are not earning. We are partnering. Notice we are not trying to get more money. This is us partnering with God in what we believe.

To recap, we have just discussed how belief is created and how it operates. It's created through what you consistently hear. What I hear, I will come to believe. Belief will always move us into action. If I believe it, then I will do it. Doing it is God's method of becoming, which in turn, causes me to experience the fullness God intends. Without belief, the receiver won't get what was given; and what was given, will not be released in the earth. Belief is the support system to partnering with God. Without it, there is no partnership. Without partnership, there is no transformation.

Chapter 5: Hope–the Transporter

INTRODUCTION

We have discussed both the beginning and the support system to the Process of Faith. We have learned that grace is the beginning and the Initiator of the process. Grace is God's part and it's His role in the partnership. Belief is the support system of the process. What we believe determines what we receive. What we believe determines what we will experience. If we believe it, then we will partner with God to do it.

We have covered God's part and we have begun to venture into ours. Let's continue in that vein looking at biblical hope.

THE BRIDGE

Looking back at the bridge, we can view grace and faith as the cliff sides, and belief as the support systems that give the bridge structure and stability. Grace gives, faith receives, and belief supports the partnership. Now, let's look at something we have yet to focus upon. Let's look at the delivery trucks-the vehicles that are responsible for transporting the cargo from point "A" to point "B."

It is feasible to say grace gives the cargo, faith receives the cargo, and belief supports the cargo ensuring it gets across. But what holds the cargo? What holds peace, love, provision, deliverance, or healing? What holds the things that God is giving, that we are to receive? -hope. Hope is God's personal delivery system. Hope is the shipping container through which He gives and we receive.

When we need something, we reach for the container in which that specific item is found. It's the same with spiritual principles. All that we receive in Christ is found in the container of hope. Hope is what we reach for when we are in need, and it's the container that holds God's possessions.

DEFINITION

Hope, according to Webster's Dictionary, means to cherish a desire with anticipation: to want something to happen or be true. What must be understood about this definition is it makes hope seem wishful. Someone who works within this kind of hope, isn't sure of anything and therefore is hesitant in all their doings. Biblical hope isn't a wish or a desire that something might happen. If you're wishing, or you're not sure something will happen, but you wish that it would, you are not operating in biblical hope.

Biblical hope is a confident expectation. It not wishful-it's certain. Let's break this definition apart. Webster's says that confidence is a feeling or belief that you can do something well or succeed at something. Expectation, according to Webster's, is the act or state of expecting. Anticipation is a word associated with this, so to put it simply, biblical hope deals in a certain anticipation. You know what is coming and therefore, you plan accordingly. When you're "in hope" your mind focuses on what is coming and nothing changes that fact. You are fully convinced of the approaching occurrence you are expecting. You have a confidant expectation.

IT'S COMING

Hope is the opening step towards the beginning of Faith. Faith is all about receiving what grace has given. Imagine this: You see delivery trucks coming across the bridge. A company of some kind, packed the cargo, placed it in the trucks, and sent the trucks to the company that is accepting the products. We are the receivers on that end.

Now put yourself in the position of those who are expecting their cargo. You have purchased it. You have gone through the necessary paperwork to transfer the property. Legally that product is now yours. You have every right to whatever is in that delivery truck. It has your name on it. Even though you have all authority regarding that cargo, it still hasn't shown up yet. It's either sitting in the distribution center on the other side of the bridge or it's in the truck but hasn't yet left the parking lot. Maybe the truck is in transit. It's just leaving the center, about a mile or two out. Whatever the case, that cargo is yours, it just hasn't arrived yet-but it's coming.

This is the position of those in hope. They possess what they believe for, even though they don't see it yet. The key word is yet. They know it's coming, for it has been purchased with something far precious than coin. **"Knowing that you were not redeemed with perishable things like silver or gold from your futile way of life inherited from your forefathers, but with the precious blood, as of a lamb unblemished and spotless, the blood of Christ." (1Peter 1:18-19,**

NASB). They know it belongs to them because it has been promised to them from He who will not lie. **"So that by two unchangeable things in which it is impossible for God to lie..." (Hebrews 6:18, NASB).**

Here's the situation. Grace tells us we have what is needed in Christ and belief moves us into partnering with the promise through action. As we engage in partnership, our hope awakens. We don't see the promise yet, but we know it's coming because we know Who has sent it. Because we know Who sent it, we stay stable and strong as we continue to partner with what we believe.

We are confidently expecting that what was promised is coming, that it's in transit, and that its arrival is imminent. We might not see it now, but we trust the Giver to such a degree that we know we will. Look at what Paul says about the future glory in Romans.

"For in hope we have been saved, but hope that is seen is not hope; for who hopes for what he already sees? But if we hope for what we do not see, with perseverance we wait eagerly for it." Romans 8:24-25 (NASB)

Notice the phrase, hope that is seen is not hope. If something has arrived and you can see it with your natural eyes, you no longer need to hope that it's coming. It's here. You see it right in front of you. Therefore, hope is no longer necessary. This reveals to us a very critical characteristic about hope-it's futuristic. If the thing you are believing for hasn't arrived yet, it's coming. Therefore, you stand in hope, eagerly awaiting its arrival.

Here's another characteristic about hope revealed in the above scripture. Hope is needed as long as you can't see the promise. The moment you see the thing you are hoping for with your natural eyes, then you no longer need hope and hope leaves. So fundamentally, hope is always looking for what it's expecting. It's looking in the natural for the miracle. When you go to the healing line, if you're looking for results, you are "in hope," because hope is looking for healing to show up. Faith isn't looking in the natural. It looks at what's true in the spiritual. You are already healed in Christ, so the person "in faith" calls the deal done. They aren't looking for it because they already believe they have it in the Spirit. They go to the healing line to partner with the minster, or like-minded brother or sister, to bring what is already true in the Spirit into the natural.

So, grace says I have the promise in Christ and when I believe it, I'll cooperate with it through action. As I cooperate, if I'm standing in hope, I look for the natural showings of its arrival. I see if my cough is still active, has my account changed, or do I see a difference in my child's behavior. If I'm "in faith," I don't look for anything, but accept the truth, that I have already received everything in Christ. My focus is entirely on what's true, and I'm convinced of its accuracy despite what I see before me.

HOPE VS. FAITH

Since we've already touched on it, let's discuss how hope is associated with faith. Hope was meant to be discussed alongside its partner, and it's difficult to keep them apart. Let's go to the book of Hebrews to make this point.

"Now faith is the substance of things hoped for, the evidence of things not seen." **Hebrews 11:1 (KJV)**

Let's put together all that we know about hope. Hope is a confident expectation. Those who are "in hope" are not wavering and they're not wishing. They stand strong in expectation of what is to come because their confidence is in the person who is worthy of all honor and praise. God has been found trustworthy. So, the hopeful one does not waver in his/her expectation. Hope is futuristic. The moment the thing we hope for shows up, hope is no longer needed. Hope is designed to keep us stable while the miracle is in transit. Hope is also always looking for the promise in the natural. It's expecting what it needs to show up.

So, what is faith? **"Now faith,"** **(Hebrews 11:1)** speaks of the viewpoint of those "in faith." While hope is futuristic, faith is present. While those who are "in hope" look for what's coming, those who are "in faith" look for what's already here. A person "in hope" would say concerning their healing, "My healing is coming." It's a very trusting and confident statement, but it's not "in faith." Faith is present, it's now. A person "in faith" would say, "I am healed." Do you notice the difference?

"Now faith is the substance" Not only is faith focused in the now, but faith is also substance. What is meant by substance? Substance is anything that can be seen, tasted, heard, smelled, or touched. It is the building blocks of the natural realm. Anything that can be reacted with through the senses has substance. The chair you might be sitting on has substance. The glass you might be drinking out of has substance. If you can cooperate with it in the natural realm, it has substance. All things that exist in this natural realm must have substance. So, if faith is substance, then faith makes something exist in this natural realm.

"Now faith is the substance" The substance of what? -**"of things hoped for."** Do you see why we need to understand hope before faith? Faith gives substance to the thing you cannot see in order that you might see it. Remember that when you're "in hope," you can't see that which you're expecting. It hasn't shown up yet, so you're "in hope," eagerly waiting on its arrival. When you move "in faith," you're taking the thing you can't see and giving it substance. When it has substance, it can live in this natural world. "In faith," you are taking what exists from where you can't see and making it visible where you can.

"Through faith we understand that the worlds were framed by the word of God, so that things which are seen were not made of things which do appear."
Hebrews 11:3 (KJV)

Let's quickly summarize all the characteristics of faith before we look at this from a different angle. Faith is now, not future. If I'm in faith, I have it now. I'm not going to have it or will have it⁻I already have it. Faith is substance. Through faith, I materialize what I can't see so I can see it. Knowing this, let's look at verse 3 of Hebrews 11.

How was the world created? According to Hebrews 11:3, it was through faith. Faith created what we see every day. So, with this, we now have another characteristic of faith⁻it's creative. Faith is now, it is substance, and it is creative. Who created the world? -God created the world through the Word of God, through faith. Now, who is God? **"God is spirit, and those who worship Him must worship in spirit and truth." (John 4:24, NASB).** God is a spirit. Where do spirits live? -in the spirit world. However, the spirit world is the realm of the unseen. This means that just because we can't see it, doesn't mean it doesn't exist.

God, who is a spirit, created the natural world. However, the natural world is unaware of the spiritual world without divine revelation. Think of a potter. A potter creates something outside of himself, but within his environment. The potter resides in his environment, but what he creates is not aware of the potter's world.

Here's my point. At the story of creation there were two worlds present⁻God's and ours. God in the spirit world created our natural realm from within His. He had to reach out from His home to create this one. God is a Giver. He has given all that we have need of in Christ. But a person can only give from what is in their environment. So, God can only give that which is in His environment. **"Blessed be the God and Father of our Lord Jesus Christ, who has blessed us with every spiritual blessing in the heavenly places in Christ." (Ephesians 1:3, NASB).**

The gifts God has given are spiritual, but we live in a natural world. Healing, provision, deliverance are all spiritual gifts, but when we receive them, they materialize in this natural world. So how do we get what is spiritual to show up in the natural? -through faith. Therefore, the Process of Faith, how we receive from God, how we partner with God, is represented in this book as a bridge. A bridge brings two worlds together. This is what faith does. It brings what is true in one world into existence within the next.

A bridge touches both cliff sides. Likewise, the Process of Faith must touch both arenas. To bring God's realm into ours, we must be able to utilize something that can exist in both realms. This is faith.

"For through the grace given to me I say to everyone among you not to think more highly of himself than he ought to think; but to think so as to have sound judgment, as God as allotted to each a measure of faith."
Romans 12:3 (NASB)

We see in Romans 12:3 that God has given everyone a measure of faith. This means faith originates in God. If faith originates in God, then faith exists in the spiritual realm. With that in mind, let's look at Mark 11.

"And Jesus answered saying to them, 'Have faith in God. Truly I say to you, whoever says to this mountain, 'Be taken up and cast into the sea,' and does not doubt in his heart, but believes that what he says is going to happen, it will be granted him." Mark 11:22-23 (NASB)

Faith is a spiritual force, but it also operates in this natural world. How? -through our actions. Do you remember what was said about belief? What I believe moves me into action. When you do what you believe, faith is released which causes what can't be seen to be seen.

In bringing all the characteristics of faith together-faith is now, it's substance, and it's creative. When I do what I believe, I release this spiritual force called faith. Through faith, I cause what I'm hoping for to materialize in the now. Remember, hope is future. Faith is now. Through the Process of Faith, I'm making what is true in God's realm to be true in mine. I receive what I can't see, the substance of faith, and use it to create within the realm in which I live. This is how faith works.

TO HOLD ON TO

"Through faith we understand that the worlds were framed by the word of God, so that things which are seen were not made of things which do appear."
Hebrews 11:3 (KJV)

This verse makes it clear that through faith God created from His realm to make ours. To do that, He had to reach from His into ours. How did He do that? -through faith because faith operates in both worlds. Since God can reach into the natural through faith, we can reach into the spiritual through faith. Faith is the ultimate connector between God and man. Through faith, we take what is unseen and make it visible in this realm.

When we reach into the spiritual, to what does our faith grab hold? -the thing for which we hope. If you never step into hope, you can't step into faith. And if you can't step into faith, you will never receive what grace has given. Faith grabs hold of our hope. Without hope, faith will have nothing in which to grab. Remember, if you're in hope, you believe that God has given you something you can't see. Faith specializes in making what is unseen visible. If you never choose to believe what God promises is coming, then you won't make a move to partner with it to make it arrive. If you never hope, you will never bring the promise to pass through faith.

Abraham is considered the Father of Faith. He was a man full of faith. In fact, you really can't talk about faith without mentioning him. Because he was a man of faith, he had to be a man of hope.

"In hope against hope he believed, so that he might become a father of many nations according to that which has been spoken, 'So shall your descendants be.'" Romans 4:18 (NASB)

"**In hope against hope he believed.**" What this means is first, he was "in hope." He was given a promise that he would be the father of many nations. Since he didn't have a child yet, he looked toward the future, believing that it was coming. He was fully persuaded that, He who promised, would fulfill that promise. "**And being fully assured that what God had promised, He was able also to perform.**" (Romans 4:21, NASB).

The phrase "**in hope against hope,**" refers to the fact that Abraham had to stay "in hope" against all hope. He had to remain in that posture of hope for years until Sarah became pregnant, thus seeing the beginning of the promise. He had to keep that posture throughout all situations designed to influence him otherwise. Time, the ages of both he and Sarah, and a myriad of trials were tactics that came against Abraham's hope. The question that must be asked here is how did he stay in hope? How did he not allow the impossibility of the situation to cause him to waver and move out of hope? Look at the next verse.

"Without becoming weak in faith, he contemplated his own body, now as good as dead since he was about a hundred years old, and the deadness of Sarah's womb; yet, with respect to the promise of God, he did not waver in unbelief but grew strong in faith, giving glory to God." Romans 4:19 (NASB)

What does faith hold onto? -that for which we hope. If we never step into hope, we can never step into faith. Hope is the door to faith. Hope is the container of faith. All that we are believing for is found in hope. This ultimately will move us from a posture of hope into faith where we can make what is unseen visible. How did Abraham stay «in hope?» -he didn't. He moved forward into faith.

This is what Abraham did: He began «in hope,» focusing on the character of God (grace) knowing that He would keep His promise. As Abraham maintained that posture of hope, he moved into faith. Here's the thing, those who are «in hope» and maintain that hope, at some point, get tired of looking to the future and expecting it to come. Eventually, by design, they move into the idea that this is for me now. At that moment, they make the transition into faith.

Why is this important? Because the promise isn't received by hope. It's received by faith. If something that is coming, which is the mindset of hope, is always coming-it never arrives. Remember, the moment it arrives, and you can see it, it stops being hope. You don't need hope if you can see it. Faith takes what is coming «in hope» and brings it into your now. While it is in your now, you can enjoy it, work with it, touch it, hear it, taste it, sense it.

HOPE TO FAITH

Let's say I'm waiting on a gift to arrive from a store. The posture I'm currently in is hope. I can't see it yet, but because I've purchased it, I'm confident it belongs to me. I know it's coming. The moment it arrives on my doorstep, hope leaves because I don't need hope anymore. You don't hope for something you can see. I have transitioned into faith. Have I picked it up from off of the porch yet? Have I opened the box to see if it is what I bought? -no, not yet. But I know that what I have been "in hope" for has come. Even though I haven't opened it up and checked on the box's contents naturally, I know what it contains. No one can convince me otherwise. I've received that for which I've hoped.

This is the example of the transition from hope to faith. This is also where people miss it. Since faith is seeing, they think they must see the promise in the natural before they can step into faith. Faith gives you vision, not the other way around. Faith sees the promise as true in the spirit, not the natural. Therefore, faith can bring what is true in the spirit and bring it into the natural.

If you see a promise as coming to fruition in your life now-you're in faith. If you only see it as something in the future, or in the process of coming, you are still "in hope." This isn't bad because you must have hope before you move into faith. It must be coming before it arrives, but you can't enjoy what has never come.

Let me highlight this another way. What has changed when you move from hope to faith, and therefore the thing that causes the shift, is what you believe. Remember, your belief is the supporter of our partnership with God. It determines what you receive. When you move from hope to faith, you do it through what you believe. When your belief shifts, your understanding changes. Your awareness changes. You start to realize the thing that you have been looking for, has always been here, in the now, in Christ. When this becomes real to you, no one can change your mind. You have shifted from believing something is coming, to you already having it in the now. You have moved from hope to faith.

I've shown you how we move from hope to faith by a natural expression through an expected gift arriving in the mail. Let me show you how it works in a church setting or in spiritual matters. It's the same process, but it looks a bit different. Let's say I was in an accident and I broke my leg. I'm in pain and I need healing.

Where do we start? -grace! I know that God loves me, and I know that the broken leg isn't His will, so I step into belief that healing is in Christ; and because I'm in Christ, I have my healing. Now, it's difficult for me to believe that I'm healed because of all the pain and limitations I am experiencing-not to mention, all the voices that keep saying that my life will be forever changed because of my leg. So, it's hard to say, "I am healed," like someone "in faith." But I can say, "My healing is coming," like someone who has hope.

It's important to note here, that voices from family members and friends can take a toll on your hope and faith stances. They can influence what you believe, and therefore receive. If you need to, remove them from the process. This is your life, not theirs. It is your inheritance to contend for what God has promised. I'm not suggesting that you cut them out of your life but set a firm boundary of what they can speak into or how much they can say. It's clearly best to keep the door closed on that subject and only process verbally with someone of like faith or belief.

Now as a person "in hope," I'm transitioning from hope to faith. I'm moving from seeing that it's coming to seeing I have it now in Christ. How do I do that? -through choosing what I allow to influence me. I choose what words I allow in my ears. I choose what thoughts I allow in my head. I choose what images I allow before my eyes. The enemy would want nothing more than to keep you from receiving God's promise, so he'll provide an opportunity for that religious family member to come over. He'll make it easy to miss your prayer and Bible reading for a simple phone call. If he can do anything to hinder your faith-he will. The phone call isn't bad in itself, but if it replaces your time with God and removes you from your stance of hope or faith, the devil has thwarted your plans. **"The thief comes only to steal and kill**

**and destroy; I came that they may have life and have it abundantly."
(John 10:10, NASB).**

As I spend time before God and in His Word, slowly, but surely, I start to transition from hope to faith-from seeing it in my future, to seeing it in my now.

BIBLE EXAMPLE

Let's look at a scenario in the Gospels where a person transitioned from hope to faith to receive a miracle.

"Now a certain man was sick, Lazarus of Bethany, the village of Mary and her sister Martha. It was the Mary who anointed the Lord with ointment, and wiped His feet with her hair, whose brother Lazarus was sick. So, the sister sent word to Him, saying, 'Lord, behold, he whom You love is sick.' But when Jesus heard this, He said, 'This sickness is not to end in death, but for the glory of God, so that the Son of God may be glorified by it.'" John 11:1-4 (NASB)

It's important for us to see Jesus's initial response to the information. Now if your unaware of Jesus's relationship with Lazarus, they were close friends. Jesus would spend time with Lazarus and his sisters at their house in Bethany. This wasn't simply a random person who encountered Jesus.

Look at what Jesus said the moment He received the news-this sickness will not end in death. This is His statement of faith. This is what He believes because He knows sickness is not His Father's will. How do I know it's faith and not hope? Because He explains what He knows is going to happen-not what He was expecting to happen. He wasn't merely expecting Lazarus not to die, therefore being "in hope." He knew without a shadow of doubt that Lazarus was not going to die. You could not have convinced Him otherwise.

Notice that Jesus was nowhere near Lazarus and the situation. He couldn't rely on His eyes to determine what He believed. In fact, He didn't allow what He might see to determine what He believed. A person "in hope," is looking for the promise to show up, while a person "in faith" already sees it as true in the spirit. If it's true, it's a done deal and that's not going to change. A person "in hope," is focused on the promise showing up in the natural, but a person "in faith," has received it already as something accomplished through the spirit. Jumping ahead, let's see hope and faith compared between two other people.

"Martha, therefore, when she heard that Jesus was coming, went to meet Him, but Mary stayed at the house. Marth then said to Jesus, 'Lord, if You had been here, my brother would not have died. Even now I know that whatever You ask of God, God will give You.' Jesus said to her, 'Your brother will rise again.' Martha said to Him, 'I know that he will rise again in the resurrection on the last day.' Jesus said to her, 'I am the resurrection and the life; he who believes in Me will live even if he dies, and everyone who lives and believes in Me will never die. Do you believe this?' She said to Him, 'Yes, Lord; I have believed that You are the Christ, the Son of God, even He who comes in the world.'"
John 11:20-27 (NASB)

At the beginning of their meeting, we see that Martha accepted that Lazarus was dead. However, she believed that Jesus could change things. She understood that whatever Jesus asked, God would grant. Because she believed that Jesus was the Christ, she believed that God would give whatever Christ asked.

Here is the hope part: When Jesus replied that Lazarus would rise again, Martha was looking to the future, expecting him to rise on the last day. She fully expected this to happen. She was certainly "in hope," but a shift took place-Jesus said that He is the resurrection.

Remember, a belief can lead you toward another belief. Because Martha already believed that Jesus was the Christ, when Jesus told her He was the resurrection, and that anyone who believed on Him would not die, she grabbed hold of it immediately. How do I know that she agreed with it? She said yes when Jesus asked her if she believed. Then she left the conversation to go get her sister. She ended the conversation. What's left to talk about when it's a settled matter? To Martha, it was a done deal. She moved from expecting something to happen in the future, to believing it had happened. She moved from hope to faith.

What caused the transition? -the revelation of Christ. The Word of God birthed in her the belief necessary for her to change her position. Belief moves us from hope to faith. It happened with Martha, and it can happen to you.

As we move to the next chapter, keep in mind these crucial aspects of hope. Hope is futuristic. If you are confidently expecting for something to show up, then you are "in hope." Hope also looks for the promise to be visible in the natural. Hope wants to see it. Hope is constantly looking for it, expecting it. Faith on the other hand, is now focused. Faith isn't looking for the promise. It possesses it already. While hope is trying to see it in the natural, faith sees it as finished in the spiritual. Because it operates in both realms-the unseen and the seen-it's the perfect tool to take what is true in the unseen and cause it to be visible in the seen. What causes the transition from hope to faith? -what you believe. As your belief changes, your progress changes. You move from hope to faith.

I want to take this time to encourage those of you who are "in hope." Do not let someone make you think you have failed because you're "in hope" and haven't yet moved into faith. Yes, your miracle is received through faith, but hope is the gateway. You're almost there. It's coming. It's on the way. Don't give up. Take the principles of faith we will cover in the next chapter and make the transition. You shall see your miracle.

Chapter 6: Faith–the Receiver

INTRODUCTION

We have arrived at the other side of the bridge! We covered the other cliffside, the support system of the bridge, and the delivery system of the cargo. Grace has given what is needed, belief has determined and supported it, and hope is transporting it my direction. The next step in the Process of Faith is to lay hold of the promise and receive it fully.

In the previous chapter, we studied the concept of hope. We learned that hope is a natural focus where we confidently expect for God's goodness to show up. Whether it's healing, provision, deliverance, wisdom, love, joy, or anything else in God's glorious possession, hope is constantly looking for the promise to arrive. It's futuristic in design, looking ahead to what is expected. Eventually, hope will make the transition into faith⁻ from looking for it in the natural, to a mentality of owning it in the spiritual.

FROM OLD TO NEW

Let's look now at the covenant we live under. Remember, the covenant, or agreement of the day, is what defines our partnership with God. It determines and provides the guidelines in how we receive what God is giving.

If you recall, under the Old Covenant, the Jews had to do (or act) first to be blessed. God's blessings were withheld due to their disobedience. His desires could only be experienced if His people earned it through following the Law. Remember, the purpose of the Law was to bring the Jews to the understanding that they needed God. We have found out through James 2:10-11, that if they disobeyed any part of the Law, then they were guilty of it in its entirety. That sense of guilt, if properly understood and received, would reveal that they needed help. They needed a Savior.

We also learned through the "Sermon on the Mount," that even if they followed the physical requirements of the Law, which they could never fully do, they would still be in violation of the spiritual meaning behind the Law. Just because they could keep themselves from killing someone, didn't mean they could keep themselves from hating someone (Matthew 5:21-26). This principle of truth emanates from the fullness of God's heart.

So, here's the question behind it all. If the Jews weren't blessed until they obeyed, and it was impossible for them to be fully obedient due to their fallen nature, how were they blessed at all? It seems the whole system was stacked against them.

I call what we are about to explore God's loophole. He loves His people, and because of His nature, He wants to give to them. The problem is, the Old Covenant required them to earn what they received from God, and since they couldn't, they placed God in a hard position. He would either have to accept that He would never be able to reveal His love to His people

85

again or, establish a method in which they were forgiven for their transgressions, thus liberating Him to bless them. So, He established the sacrificial system.

"Then the LORD spoke to Moses, saying, 'Speak to the sons of Israel, saying, "If a person sins unintentionally in any of the things which the LORD has commanded not to be done, and commits any of them, if the anointed priest sins so as to bring guilt on the people, then let him offer to the Lord a bull without defect as a sin offering for the sin he has committed.... Thus, the priest shall make atonement for him in regard to his sin which he has committed, and he will be forgiven.'" **Leviticus 4:1-3, 35 (NASB)**

When the Law is broken its called sin. The word sin means to miss the mark. It's like hitting a target. If you miss the target, or the goal, then you have missed the mark. You have sinned. God doesn't want us to hurt one another, so if you slander another person, you have missed the mark or the goal. You have sinned.

Disobedience to the Law made one undeserving of being blessed. Remember, this was a covenant. What happened when this covenant, which was a blood covenant, was broken? -death. What was required? -a life for a life. **"For the wages of sin is death..." (Romans 6:23, NASB).** God, who is extremely merciful, didn't want to bring that kind of justice, so He instituted the sacrifices. This meant an animal would die in the place of the person. The animal took the place of the individual, taking upon itself the sin that was committed. When it was killed, the sin was killed with it. With that specific sin taken care of, the person was then free from the penalty of that action. The penalty was taken by the animal, allowing the person to be blessed.

The entire point of the sacrificial system was to release forgiveness. Forgiveness is the main thing sought after when you have wronged someone. This was God saying, "I forgive you for your sin-the action that missed the mark." After forgiveness had been granted, blessings could be transferred.

Without forgiveness, the penalty of sin (death) had not been paid. Therefore, the sinner was still deserving of death.

Sacrifices were to be done for each and every situation or sin that could be committed. The book of Leviticus is full of these examples. The fact that it's lengthy and deep speaks to the seriousness nature of dealing with sin. The question we must ask in all of this is, "What does this have to do with the New Covenant?"

"For the Law, since it has only a shadow of the good things to come and not the very form of things, can never, by the same sacrifices which they offer continually year by year, make perfect those who draw near. Otherwise, would they not have ceased to be offered, because the worshipers, having once been cleansed, would no longer have had consciousness of sins? By this will we have been sanctified through the offering of the body of Jesus Christ once for all. Every priest stands daily ministering and offering time after time the same sacrifices, which can never take away sins; but He, having offered one sacrifice for sins for all time, sat down at the right hand of God, waiting from that time onward until His enemies be made a footstool for His feet. For by one offering He has perfected for all time those who are sanctified."
Hebrews 10:1-2, 10-14 (NASB)

Every time someone broke the Law, a sacrifice was offered up to God so that He could release forgiveness thus liberating that person from the penalty of death. Now, free from the penalty of that sin, God could bless them. However, here's the issue: The physical act of sin was handled, but the real issue was still at hand. The sin nature, our overwhelming urge to do that which God hates, was still active. Yes, the sacrifices covered that one sin, but they could never free us from committing the sin in the first place. This was the lesson of the Law. There is a spiritual undercurrent preventing us from doing what God wants. We need help.

It wasn't necessarily the one act of sin that was at stake, it was the fact that they couldn't choose to do what God wanted. The fact that they were prone to sin revealed that they were separated from abiding in God's presence. This was the whole point God desired to reveal. You are separated from Me, and I want you back.

This is why we need Jesus! He perfectly performed the requirements of the Law. He lived life without sinning. Everything He did was on point in submission to the requirement of the Law. If you remember in Leviticus, for an animal to be a worthy sacrifice for the sins of a person, it had to be without blemish or spot. In other words, it had to be perfect.

Jesus is our spotless lamb, **"but with precious blood, as of a lamb unblemished and spotless, the blood of Christ." (1Peter 1:19, NASB)**. Through His sacrifice on the cross, Jesus took my place for all the sins I committed and would commit in this lifetime. One sacrifice for all time, for all people. He took my sins upon Himself and placed His righteousness, His right-standing before God, upon me. **"He made Him who knew no sin to be sin on our behalf, so that we might become the righteousness of God in Him." (2 Corinthians 5:21, NASB).**

Therefore, without Jesus, there is no Christianity. He did for us what we couldn't do on our own. Instead of trying to be worthy, He made us worthy. Instead of trying to be accepted, He made us accepted. Instead of trying to be loved, He revealed that we were already loved.

When I received Christ, my old life was put to death, just like Christ's body on the cross. And in the same manner in which He rose on the third day, so do I rise into a different life.

"Therefore, we have been buried with Him through baptism into death, so that as Christ was raised from the dead through the glory of the Father, so we too might walk in newness of life. For if we have become united with Him in the likeness of His death, certainly we shall also be in the likeness of His resurrection, knowing this, that our old self was crucified with Him, in order that our body of sin might be done away with, so that we would no longer be slaves to sin; for he who has died is freed from sin." Romans 6:4-7 (NASB)

"Therefore, if anyone is in Christ, he is a new creature; the old things passed away; behold, new things have come." 2 Corinthians 5:17 (NASB)

Because I have a different life, I have a different nature. The sin nature, that prevented me from doing what God wanted, has been removed and has been replaced with Christ's nature. Before Christ, I had no power over sin. In Christ, I'm free to choose. And because of Him and His love for me, why would I ever choose anything that He wouldn't want for me. Under the Old Covenant, I was forced to comply to my sinful nature. Under the New Covenant, I'm liberated. I choose to lay my life down for Him who laid His life down for me. The sixth chapter of Romans reiterates this point. It lays the foundations of been set free from sin and the old nature.

"Do you not know that when you present yourselves to someone as slaves for obedience, you are slaves of the one whom you obey, either of sin resulting in death, or of obedience resulting in righteousness? But thanks be to God that through you were slaves of sin, you became obedient from the heart to that form of teaching to which you were committed, and having been freed from sin, you became slaves of righteousness." Romans 6:16-18 (NASB)

I have been set free from my obligated obedience to sin. Now, I can live the life Christ lived and the life God always wanted me to have.

Earlier, I mentioned that Christ is the Initiator and the Originator of all things to the Christian. We have now come full circle. We worship Him because of all that He has done. Under the Old Covenant, actions moved Him. Under the New Covenant, His actions have moved me. His love moves me to love. His giving influences me to give. He is the example I choose to follow.

This is also why I am able to live righteously and overcome every sin. Jesus overcame for me and shows me how. You might be thinking, Nathan sinning is just a way of life.

It's human nature. Yes, in our old life that's true, but not now. We no longer live a normal human life because of what Christ has done. Quit living under your potential and become the ultimate example of God's grace! Jesus said to the woman caught in adultery, **"From now on sin no more."** **(John 8:11, NASB).** He said this under the Old Covenant, how much more weighted is this to those graced as we are under the New?

I'm not trying to hammer you, but rather encourage you on toward liberation. You don't have to keep doing the thing you hate. You hate it and God hates it. Partner with Him to fully eliminate it. He has already accomplished all that is needed, now partner with Him through faith to see it come to fruition. It won't happen overnight; it takes time for your belief to be brought into alignment. But once your belief system has come into agreement with Christ and His actions on the cross, you will do what you believe and eventually see what you believe. Remember it's a process, not an equation.

This is the covenant we navigate in our partnership with God. Under the Old Covenant, He didn't give until we obeyed. In Christ, we hear God the Father declare to all mankind, "Never again will I allow my love to be dictated by your obedience. I shall love you and give to you regardless of you. It will be up to you on whether you see it in your life."

This is the main point of this book. My actions are not preventing Him from giving. My actions are preventing me from receiving. He has already given all things in Christ. If I'm not seeing them, it's not His fault, it's mine. It's in my account, it's up to me to cash it in.

Before we go any further, I want to make something abundantly clear. Yes, Christ's actions under the Law and at the cross liberated me from a sin trapped life. He set me free enabling me to choose, and now I'm no longer a slave to sin. Because I'm now in Christ, I have all the gifts and blessings that are His. It's an amazing thought to realize the tremendous blessings we have been given, but let me remind us here to be careful not to honor the gifts outside of their place.

Here's my point. The main focal point of the Gospel is this: I was away from Him, and I was going to Hell. My sin nature, my inability to choose God's way, forever kept me from Him and therefore, kept me from relationship with Him. On the cross, Jesus removed the barrier that separated me from my Father, opening the door for me to come home. He has removed the veil so that I might fellowship with my Father. This is where He wanted me all along.

Yes, the Gospel heals me, provides for me, delivers me from all my mistakes, and breaks my chains, but never allow the fruit to overshadow the tree. I'm no longer going to Hell, and I shall live in eternity with Jesus. That, my friends, is worth more than everything else I can receive from Him. Everything else is part of the package that is Christ. I have Him and that needs to be enough. It's not enough for Him because He is just that good. He wants me whole and sound. He wants me to gradually become what I already am in Christ. But the moment the provision becomes more important than the blood, that is an issue. We've traded Jesus for what He gives. This is always damaging in any relationship. It makes you a taker rather than a receiver.

I caution you in this: This is a battle that all believers will face. We must remember that God Himself is the reason-not what He gives. We must maintain that posture for the advancement of His kingdom so others might experience what we enjoy in Him. I'm not saying don't receive abundance, because God has it for you. Just make sure that abundance doesn't become your god. The gift should never replace the Giver.

Just like the Abrahamic and the Old, each covenant had a policy of agreement, where all the roles were laid out. In closing of this section, let's look at the New Covenant's roles.

"For this is the covenant that I will make with the House of Israel. After those days, says the Lord; I will put my laws into their minds, and I will write them on their hearts. And I will be their God, and they shall be my people. And they shall not teach everyone his fellow citizen, and everyone his brother, saying, 'Know the Lord,' For all will know Me, From the least to the greatest of them. For I will be merciful to their iniquities, And I will remember their sins no more."
Hebrews 8:10-12 (NASB)

Did you see anything in that portion of scripture that lays out a to do list? I Under this covenant, God has taken the whole weight of the it upon His shoulders. Remember, under the Old Covenant, He had to depend on His people to stay true to their part for Him to stay true to His. He decided not to go through that again.

Who were the subjects of the agreement within the Old Covenant? -God and man. How did Jesus show Himself to us? -as a man. Jesus is our representative. Jesus, who was fully God and fully man, fulfilled the obligations we couldn't keep. After Jesus' death and resurrection, God established a New Covenant with man's representative. He made an agreement between Himself and Christ. If God keeps His part, and Christ, our human representative, keeps His, the agreement is binding. And since God always keeps His part, and as Jesus walked the earth, He kept His perfectly to the letter, the covenant is forever established.

So, what do we do to get in on it? We receive Christ's part as our own. We receive His efforts as our efforts through faith. Jesus represents me in the covenant. My disobedience doesn't hinder God from blessing me because it's not my obedience that is on the line for the covenant to take effect-it's Christ's. My obedience isn't required for God to bless me, but it is required for me to receive what God is giving. God gave to Christ and, since I'm in Christ, I'm a beneficiary of the covenant. However, what I do determines what I receive "in Christ." It's a partnership.

RECEIVING CHRIST

We have seen the guidelines of the New Covenant. We have seen that Christ completed the requirements of the Law and therefore fulfilled the Old Covenant. His actions on the cross, not only liberated us from the law of sin and death but, brought us into a new life with a new nature-enabling us with the ability to choose God's ways. **"For the law of the Spirit of life in Christ Jesus has set you free from the law of sin and of death." (Romans 8:2, NASB).** While we are learning how to live our new lives in Christ, becoming Christ-like, God doesn't want our transformation to prevent Him from lavishing His love upon us. So, He has given all things in Christ and as we remain in Christ, we possess all that grace has made available.

Remember, we are examining faith, the receiving end of the Process of Faith. This is how we lay hold of what God has made available to us through Christ. How do we receive God's blessings? How did we receive Christ? Jesus is the possessor of all God wants for us. By receiving Christ, we receive everything. So, how you received Christ, is exactly how you receive healing, prosperity, deliverance, soundness of mind, wisdom, joy, peace, love, whatever is needed. Let's go to a verse that we commonly use to discuss belief and take it further.

"...for 'Whoever will call on the Name of the Lord will be saved.' How then will they call on Him in whom they have not believed? How will they believe in Him whom they have not heard? And how will they hear without a preacher? How will they preach unless they are sent? Just as it is written, "How beautiful are the feet of those who bring good news of good things!' However, they did not all heed the good news; for Isaiah says, 'Lord, who has believed our report?' So, faith comes from hearing, and hearing by the word of Christ."
Romans 10:13-17 (NASB)

This is how we are saved: A preacher is sent with the Gospel. He preaches the Gospel. We hear the message. We believe it. That belief moves us into partnering with it which births salvation. What made salvation available? -grace! Because God loves you, He isn't going to allow your actions to hinder Him from giving the greatest gift He could possibly give to you. Grace gives it. We hear it. We believe the message. Our belief moves us into agreement with the truth. Salvation is produced.

Focus on verse 17 for the moment. **"So, faith comes from hearing, and hearing by the word of Christ." (Romans 10: 17, NASB).** This entire portion of scripture is centered around belief, but when we get to verse 17, faith is introduced.

Belief is closely related to faith. Belief moves us into acting upon what we believe. If I believe it, then I will do it. So, when does belief become faith? -belief is a verb while faith is a noun. Belief moves us into action, but faith is what is created because of that action. Just like hope is the gateway to faith, belief is the support system of faith. Without belief, action cannot take place, and without an action of belief (faith as a spiritual force), it can't be released to make what is unseen visible.

"Even so, faith, if it has no works, is dead, being by itself. But someone may well say, 'You have faith and I have works; show me your faith without the works, and I will show you my faith by my works.' You believe that God is one. You do well, the demons also believe, and shudder. But are you willing to recognize, you foolish fellow, that faith without works is useless?"
James 2:17-20 (NASB)

The book of James teaches us that faith without works is dead. If faith doesn't have works to support it, it's useless. It's not able to do that which it was designed to do. Look at verse 18. **"But someone may well say, 'You have faith and I have works; show me your faith without the works, and I will show you my faith by my works.'" (James 2:18, NASB).** Notice James says I will show you my faith by my works. What we do reveals our faith. The spiritual power of faith isn't revealed until it is produced by works.

So, when we hear the Gospel, and believe it, our belief will move us to partnership. This action releases faith, producing salvation. This is how we received Christ and it is how we receive everything else as well.

FAITH RELEASED

Grace makes everything available. We hear about it and believe it. Belief creates actions that release faith to lay hold of what grace has made available. So, what actions release our faith? Hopefully the case has been made that what we believe will cause us to move into agreement with Heaven which releases the faith necessary to lay hold of what God has given in Christ. What do I do to release my faith?

Faith is released through actions. These actions are a response to what we believe. If I need healing, my belief that Christ is my healing and that I already have my healing in Christ, will lead me into an action of agreement to partner with that belief. When you were saved, what did the minister or the individual that led you to the Lord have you do? They had you pray a prayer. In other words, they had you speak in agreement what you believed to be true. You believed it, so you partnered with it through your words. The first action produced will be what I say. My speech is the first action I use to show my agreement in what I believe.

In James 2:18 we read, **"But someone may well say, 'You have faith and I have works; show me your faith without the works, and I will show you my faith by my works.'" (James 2:18, NASB).** James lets us know that faith is visible. You can tell if someone is in faith because the first indicator of that faith is their words.

Do you remember what Jesus asked Martha when He told her that He was the resurrection? **"Jesus said to her, 'I am the resurrection and the life; he who believes in Me will live even if he dies, and everyone who lives and believes in Me will never die. Do you believe this?'" (John 11:25-26, NASB).** He asked for her agreement. What did she do to show her belief (her agreement)? -she spoke. What she said showed her agreement with what Jesus was saying. Why did she agree? -because she believed. Her belief moved her to speak. **"But having the same spirit of faith, according to what is written, 'I believed; therefore, I spoke,' we also believe; therefore, we also speak." (2 Corinthians 4:13, NASB).**

So, when you are in the middle of a situation that requires your partnership with God, the first thing you do is take stock in what you say. What you believe will come out in your speech. What you say will reveal what you believe.

"...that if you confess with your mouth Jesus as Lord and believe in your heart that God raised Him from the dead, you will be saved; for with the heart a person believes, resulting in righteousness, and with the mouth he confesses, resulting in salvation." Romans 10:9-10 (NASB)

The word confess, means to say the same as. In other words, when you are confessing, you are copying the speech of another. When you copy the speech of another, you are in full agreement. According to Romans 10:9, when I confess Jesus as Lord and believe in my heart that God raised Him from the dead, then I'm saved. My belief shows itself by influencing my speech to agree with what God has already said.

Romans 10:10 tells us that it is with the heart a person believes. What this says is that belief is birthed out of the heart. Now take that and add it to what Jesus said in Matthew 12:34, **"You brood of vipers, how can you, being evil, speak what is good? For the mouth speaks out of that which fills the heart." (Matthew 12:34, NASB).** Belief comes out of the heart and since what my heart is filled with is released through my mouth, what I say is an indication of what I believe.

When I'm in a pressure-packed situation, the weight of that moment will cause what I believe to come out from my heart through my mouth. What I believe will either release faith or fear. I'll either partner with God or the enemy. So, the question that must be asked is, "If I don't like what I believe, how do I change it? How do I change the contents of my heart, so that my belief filled words will release faith and not fear? Let's go back to Romans 10:13-17.

"...for 'Whoever will call on the Name of the Lord will be saved.' How then will they call on Him in whom they have not believed? How will they believe in Him whom they have not heard? And how will they hear without a preacher? How will they preach unless they are sent? Just as it is written, 'How beautiful are the feet of those who bring good news of good things!' However, they did not all heed the good news; for Isaiah says, 'Lord, who has believed our report?' So, faith comes from hearing, and hearing by the word of Christ."
Romans 10:13-17 (NASB)

How did I come to believe? -I heard. What you hear goes into your heart. If I have an empty glass, and I continue to pour water into it, what will happen? -it will run over. If the glass is a cup and I can't see through it, then the outpour reveals to me what has been poured into it. Likewise, what I say is a direct indication of what is in my heart. What I say tells others what I have been listening to, because what I have heard is what I have come to believe. This is important! It doesn't take one small pour to create a run over. No, it's a consistent pouring that causes the contents to spill over. Likewise, it's what you hear and hear and hear, consistently, that will establish the abundance of your heart. In turn, that abundance will spill over into your words.

It's not one bad statement that causes the difference. It's the consistency of bad statements that causes the difference.

So, my point is this: What you say and what you hear go hand in hand. Your words are still going through your ears, going down into your heart, establishing what you believe, influencing your actions to release faith or fear. Your partnership with God hinges on what you have been hearing and by what you have been saying.

We have established that your words are the first action in the release of your faith. But what are the others? To put it simply, the other actions are what comes out of what you believe. It sounds vague, but it's the truth. If I believe it, I will do it. It's that simple. If I believe that God is my source, then I will give. If I believe that God is my health, then I'm healed. If I believe that God is my freedom, then I'm free.

What I believe will determine what I do and is the direct result of what is filling my ears. Manage what you listen to and manage what you do. Let's add another dimension to this.

"But prove yourselves doers of the word, and not merely hearers who delude themselves. For if anyone is a hearer of the word and not a doer, he is like a man who looks at his natural face in a mirror; for once he has looked at himself and gone away, he has immediately forgotten what kind of person he was. But one who looks intently at the perfect law, the law of liberty, and abides by it, not having become a forgetful hearer but an effectual doer, this man will be blessed in what he does." James 1:22-25 (NASB)

What you listen to, is what you will come to believe. What you believe is what you will come to do. According to James 1:22-25, what you do, you will become. This is critical to living the transformed life that Christ wants for us. What we believe will affect what we do, which in turn effects who we become.

Now with this, we can easily entertain the idea that we are what we do. This is not true. But Nathan you said, we become what we do. That is correct, but identity is not based on who you become, identity is based on who you are. Identity is not what I do, but what God has called me. He calls me chosen, adopted, loved, holy, provided for, healed, whole, worthy. These qualities are what God calls me because these qualities are all found in Jesus. Truthfully, Jesus is my identity!

So, what would happen, if I listened to messages and confessed what God says about me daily? -eventually, this effects my belief about myself, and what I believe, I do, and when I do what I believe, I become what I believe. This is the Christian reality. This is how we become what we already are through faith.

Chapter 7: Prayer–the Architect

INTRODUCTION

We are now at the last step in the Process of Faith. We have ventured to discover how God partners with us and how we partner with Him. We have learned about grace and that God views us through that lens. He loves us. He wants to be a part of our lives, much like a Father and his child. Grace is the beginning of the process. It is the Initiator of the partnership. When we begin to receive from God, we begin on God's end of the partnership. We focus on His giving nature. How He sees us is what ensures that we can trust Him and thus work with Him. His character and nature assure us that He is for us, and all things are for our benefit. Christ is our example. What He has done and is doing is what enables us to work alongside Him.

We learned that belief is the supporter to the entire process. What I believe determines what I receive. My belief moves me into action. It determines whether I'm present to partner with God or not. If I don't believe it, I won't do it.

We learned that when our belief moves us into action, we first go through the door of hope. Because we believe that God is for us, and He has promised great things for us, we believe that He isn't lying. As people of hope, we look for the cargo that hope holds-believing that its arrival is assured.

Eventually, our hope is grabbed. The thing that we have believed for has become real to us. What was coming has arrived even though we don't see it in the natural. What is true in the spiritual has become real to us. We believe this, we partner with this, our actions release our faith to lay hold of it and bring what is unseen into our reality. What was once given has been received.

We have gone through many tokens of truth with one thing remaining.

THE BRIDGE

Throughout the entire project, we have used a picture the Lord gave me at the beginning of this adventure. One last time, let me explain it. It was a bridge set between two cliff sides with delivery trucks moving from the left to the right. The cliffside on the left is represented by grace, giving the product in the trucks. The left cliffside is the receiver, our faith which receives the cargo. The nails and the other support systems of the bridge ensure its stability and structure. Belief is the supporter to the entire process. The delivery trucks, carrying the cargo, represent hope. Hope not only holds that which we are believing for, it's also what brings it to us.

With every good bridge, there is a good architect behind its development. The architect is responsible for ensuring that the bridge fits the terrain in which it is being placed. Each bridge is different because each area that houses it is different. This tells us that the planning that leads to the construction is where we find the success or failure of the bridge.

In our Christian walk, what do you think would be responsible for the success or the failure of the Process of Faith? -prayer. Prayer is the key to a successful partnership with God. It is in the prayer closet where you discuss with the Author and the Finisher of our faith how He wants to proceed. Without prayer, we wouldn't know how the process is being catered to our specific situation. This is essential to a beneficial experience.

PURPOSE

Now, I'm not and have never been an architect. I have no experience or knowledge to back up my next statement. Still, when I think about the job of an architect, I suspect that each detail is designed with a purpose in mind. I believe God designs the same way. **"The LORD has made everything for its own purpose..." (Proverbs 16:4, NASB).** Everything He has done has been for a purpose. He has mapped everything out and is very specific in all His doings.

Just look at the organization of His plan for salvation. It took years and years, involving many players, with multiple backgrounds and beliefs, yet it came to fruition just like He planned. He is the ultimate tactician and He is all too willing to bring His knowledge to our aid. Prayer is how He relays His plans to us. Through conversation and dialogue, we develop a relationship with our Creator, in which He reveals the ultimate purpose of our creation. Let's look at a conversation God had with Abraham when His plans were discussed.

"And the LORD said, 'The outcry of Sodom and Gomorrah is indeed great, and their sin is exceedingly great. I will go down now and see if they have done entirely according to its outcry, which has come to Me; and if not, I will know.' Then the men turned away from there and went toward Sodom, while Abraham

was still standing before the LORD. Abraham came near and said, 'Will You indeed sweep away the righteous with the wicked? Suppose there are fifty righteous within the city; will You indeed sweep it way and not spare the place for the sake of the fifty righteous who are in it? Far be it from You to do such a thing, to slay the righteous with the wicked, so that the righteous and the wicked are treated alike. Far be it from You! Shall not the Judge of all the earth deal justly?' So, the LORD said, 'If I find in Sodom fifty righteous within the city, then I will spare the whole place on their account.'" **Genesis 18:20-26 (NASB)**

I love this story, mainly because it's a perfect example of communication with God. Here is a recap of what we are dealing with: There is a city filled with sin. An outcry comes from the city regarding the sin that is committed. God plans to do an investigation of sorts to determine the validity of the outcry.

Abraham encounters two angels on their way to investigate the city. Abraham has recently come into covenant with God. He has just entered partnership. So, what happens when your partner is about to do something? -the other partner gets to share in the conversation and offer his opinion.

This story reveals the nature of covenant and therefore, partnership. You get to discuss the inner workings of the dealings. Look at the language Abraham used with God. It's respectful because He still knows to whom he is speaking, but it still has a strong stance of opinion. Abraham isn't afraid to let his stance be made known. Those steeped in religion would have a problem with this. "God is God. How dare you question Him!" Those who think this way have no understanding of partnership. Yes, God is God! But He, as God, desires to work with us, not simply lord Himself over us. He has always wanted a relationship with us not a dictatorship like so many wrongly believe.

Let's dissect this and see how God speaks with Abraham. In Abraham's discussion with God, God was all too willing to agree with Abraham in saying, **"If I find in Sodom fifty righteous within the city, then I will spare the whole place on their account."**

(Genesis 18:26, NASB). See how He agrees with Abraham, as if to encourage the interaction. Notice that Abraham starts with one number and God agrees. Abraham lowers the number and God agrees. With this, the pattern continues. If God desired, He could easily have ended the conversation and decided on a specific number in which He wouldn't destroy the city. But that's not what He did. He answered the questions given and waited on His partner's opinion. He didn't take over the dialogue. He communicated with Abraham. He did not dictate orders.

Take the time and pay attention to the dialogue. Picture a God so interested in the opinions of His covenant partner that His actions were moved according to what was discussed. Abraham, taking his position within the relationship, sets the terms in which God would operate. Could God have disagreed and done something else? -of course! But what kind of partnership would that be if God simply dictated everything His way. God's ways are always best. His ways are higher than our ways, but He wants to teach us what those ways are and how to choose them over our own. In that, He teaches us to partner rightly.

We see examples of God allowing His people to choose throughout the Old Covenant. There were times when God didn't want to do something, but He submitted to the desires of His people. An example of this would be when Israel wanted a king to rule over them. Remember that God warned Israel against having a king, but they chose it anyway. God warned but didn't override their decision. He is still doing the same thing today. Why?- because God desires to work with you, not over you.

This is what it means to pray. It's a dialogue between you and Him. It's communication between two parties, discussing matters of importance. In prayer, both you and God should be participating within the discussion. If you are the only one talking, God's thoughts aren't being received. His ideas are far more vital.

Communication is the backbone for each partnership and prayer is how we converse with our covenant partner. Cooperation with God is greatly hindered without prayer. When dialogue is lacking, plans can't be discussed. If plans aren't discussed, you will either do something you wish you hadn't, or you will avoid something you wish you had pursued. Prayer is communication, and without it, fruitful activity is hindered.

Let's look at another popular story to explain cooperation through communication.

"Now when it was evening, the disciples came to Him and said, 'This place is secluded and the hour is already past to eat; send the crowds away, so that they may go into the villages and buy food for themselves.' But Jesus said to them, 'They do not need to go; you give them something to eat!' They said to Him, 'We have nothing here except five loaves and two fish.' And He said, 'Bring them here to Me.' And ordering the crowds to sit down on the grass, He took the five loaves and the two fish, and looked up towards heaven. He blessed the food and breaking the loaves, He gave them to the disciples and the disciples gave them to the crowds. And they all ate and were satisfied, and they picked up what was left over of the broken pieces: twelves full baskets. There were about five thousand men who ate, besides women and children."
Matthew 14:15-21 (NASB)

Notice how Jesus and the disciples spoke with one another. The disciples presented their opinions to Christ, who then presented His own. Notice that the disciples submitted to Jesus' idea. You might be thinking, of course they did! It's Christ! But how many times has God suggested something to us and we went another direction? Take a moment and try to remember a couple of those times. Did God chase after you demanding you change your course? -of course not. He waited for you to realize that His way is better after all.

After the submission came the instruction. The disciples did everything Christ instructed, and through obedience to the instruction, they experienced the miraculous. I think sometimes we make the miraculous complicated. Could it be that miracles materialize just by us doing what God says? Listening to His instruction, submitting our steps to His voice, and offering our hands to His work. That was how the disciples did it. I'm sure it's the same with us today. And how was all of this done? -through communication and dialogue.

Here's the best part about this story in my opinion: Not only did Christ instruct, but He participated with His disciples. Jesus received the bread and fish, blessed it, and gave it to the disciples who began to distribute the food throughout the crowd. Look at what happened. Christ empowered the work, then gave the work to the disciples who performed the work. Did you notice whose hands multiplied the bread and the fish? -the disciples. This wasn't a Jesus miracle. This was a miracle that Jesus and the disciples did together as a team-as partners.

This shows us such an important aspect to partnering with God in accordance with His plan. His plans aren't to prove how great He is, even though they surely do that, but to bring you into the middle of His greatness to experience it for yourself. Why? So, you can learn to do it too. This is what partnership is about with God. It's not just about doing, but learning and believing. And what happens when we come to believe something? -when we believe it, we do it. And when we do what we believe, we become what we believe. Partnership is how God changes you into His likeness-through experiencing Him. Partnership is how we become what we already are-like Him.

This is the reason you were created. It wasn't to be a teacher, even though that may be how it manifests. It wasn't to be a pastor, even though that may be how it manifests. It wasn't to be an architect, or a craftsman, or a politician, even though that may be how it manifests. You were created by Him, for Him, to be like Him, to share Him, with a world that needs Him.

Think about it. What would happen if you were to become like your partner? Cooperation would become more fluid. You would know how He moves and how He thinks-making it easier to move when He said move and speak when He said speak. Remember, He's the Giver and you are the receiver. Because you know Him and think like Him, it is easier for you to receive from Him-naturally, positionally, and spiritually.

Therefore, prayer is pivotal to the Christian. It's in the prayer closet where you get to know Him. It's in the prayer closet where you learn to trust Him. You don't trust Him only when He comes to your aid right in the nick of time. You trust Him when He reveals to you all the things you didn't know. All the things that He saved you from when you didn't know you were in trouble. All the times He made a way when you didn't even know you were lost. That is when you trust Him-when His background workings come to your foreground. Now guess how much of this would be revealed if you did all the talking? I imagine, if we come to God intending to converse with Him, to dig into His brain and His experiences, our prayer life would be far more fruitful. We would be stronger in our trust and ready to go when He said go. It's all done through prayer.

When you learn who He is through conversation and communication, you come to believe Him. Yes, you believed Him when you were saved, but now your belief is being brought into a different dimension, providing you with an opportunity to do things you couldn't even possibly imagine. How? -because you are "becoming." You are doing what you believe which turns you into what you believe. You are conversing with your God who invites you to work with Him. You are being positioned to receive and it's all because of prayer.

HOW TO PRAY

Let's look at how Jesus prayed and the impact it created. Throughout the Gospels, we don't have many recorded examples of Christ praying. We have a moment in which He teaches on prayer, and we have a time where He prays. Let's look at what He has to say about prayer first.

"When you pray, you are not to be like the hypocrites; for they love to stand and pray in the synagogues and on the street corners so that they may be seen by men. Truly I say to you, they have their reward in full. But you, when you pray, go into your inner room, close your door, and pray to your Father who is in secret; and your Father who sees what is done in secret will reward you. And when you are praying, do not use meaningless repetition as the Gentiles do, for they suppose that they will be heard because of their many words. So do not be like them; for your Father knows what you need before you ask Him. Pray, then, in this way: 'Our Father who is in heaven, Hallowed be Your name. Your kingdom come, Your will be done, On earth as it is in heaven. Give us this day our daily bread, And forgive us our debts, as we also have forgiven our debtors. And do not lead us into temptation, but deliver us from evil. [For Yours is the kingdom and the power and the glory forever. Amen'] For if you forgive others for their transgressions, your heavenly Father will also forgive you. But if you do not forgive others, then your Father will not forgive your transgressions." Matthew 6:5-15 (NASB)

Now, what covenant is this recorded under? -the Old. So, even though it is Christ talking, we must carefully examine what is being demonstrated. Even though it's under a different covenant, this still reveals God's heart and therefore His nature. Keep an eye out for anything that requires you to do something for God. Remember, under our covenant, we are receivers not Initiators. He is the beginning, not us. We are partnering with what He starts.

Look at verses 14 and 15 concerning forgiveness. Notice that it says we aren't forgiven unless we forgive others. God can't forgive me unless I forgive someone else. That's not how it works under the New Covenant. How was forgiveness given under the Law? -through the sacrifices. Who was my sacrifice for my transgressions? -Christ. Through Christ I received God's forgiveness. I'm already forgiven, not because of what I have done but because of what Christ has done. I'm forgiven, and because I'm forgiven, I forgive others. **"Be kind to one another, tender-hearted, forgiving each other, just as God in Christ also has forgiven you." (Ephesians 4:32, NASB).**

So how do we piece out what is New Covenant and what isn't? Ask God for the heart of what is said, not the way it is said. Don't copy the act but connect with the spirit of the matter. What is the heart behind Christ's words concerning prayer? First, prayer is a private thing, not a demonstrative thing. This doesn't mean we are not to pray in public. Again, it's the heart behind the matter. Are you praying to be popular and to grab attention, or are you praying to move and breathe in agreement with your partner?

Also, there is a reward connected to what is done in secret. Prayer in private is time that is sacrificed unto God. What does God do with sacrifices? -He lights them up for display. **"Then the fire of the LORD fell and consumed the burnt offering and the wood and the stones and the dust, and licked up the water that was in the trench. When all the people saw it, they fell on their faces; and they said, 'The LORD, HE is God; the LORD, HE is God.'" (1 Kings 18:38-39).** What you do for Him in secret, He will do through you in public. The private time is the birthing place for what God will do with you and through you in public.

Let's look specifically at what to pray. Christ tells us not to use repetitive words to be noticed. The whole point behind this explanation is the "why." Why are you praying? Don't use repetitive words so that your prayers are long or seem to be spiritually anointed and powerful.

How are we to pray? Let's look at the heart behind Christ's words. Verses 9 and 10 are about worship and establishing God's Lordship in the situation. Verses 11 through 13 get a little glitchy due to the Old Covenant speech. So, let's bring these verses into the New Covenant. Instead of praying that God would give us our daily bread and that He would forgive our trespasses, thank Him for already giving these things in Christ. Now remember, we aren't overriding what Christ is saying. We are bringing what was said from under one covenant into our own. Even though He is speaking to the disciples, He is still communicating under the Old Covenant. So, for us to benefit from what He's saying, we need to implement it in our New Covenant setting.

Here's an example of how you might pray these concepts according to the New Covenant: Lord, I thank You that Christ was my replacement, my sacrificial Lamb. Through Him I have been forgiven. I thank You for Your forgiveness. I move through it. I live in it. I partner with it. I take authority over every thought that would hinder me from receiving and walking in the fullness of what You want to bring to the earth. I thank You, Father, for that which You have already given. All my needs have been met. You are the Alpha and the Omega, the beginning, and the end. You have provided before I needed, and I receive the fullness of it right now in the Name of Jesus. Your love has manifested and will continue to manifest in my life. I will continue to see the manifestation of Your goodness in the land of the living.

That is an example of a New Covenant prayer. Just keep Christ at the beginning and move from there. He's the beginning and you partner with Him to that end.

This leads us into two of the main components of prayer: worship and thanksgiving. Worship is us establishing His Lordship and, therefore, our submission to His plans and ways. Thanksgiving, is covenantal language, establishing our dependence upon Him and assuring our loyalty. **"Be anxious for nothing, but in everything by prayer and supplication with thanksgiving let your requests be made known to God."** (Philippians 4:6, NASB).

We are anxious for nothing because He possesses all things and we establish His lordship through our petitions. By establishing His Supremacy, we are submitting to His will. Let's pair that thought with 1 John 5:14-15 (NASB), "This is the confidence which we have before Him, that, if we ask anything according to His will, He hears us. And if we know that He hears us in whatever we ask, we know that we have the requests which we have asked from Him."

We know we ask according to His will because we are in submission to His will. His will is our focus and the reason for our requests. When His will is our reason, His will is manifested in our requests. We also know His will because He has written it down in His Word. He is always talking about what He has already said. Another way we know His will is because we have learned it through prayer. Remember, it is in prayer where His heart is revealed. When His heart is revealed, His will has been found out.

So how do we pray? -we pray with a private tone. We aren't trying to be noticed, we simply reveal His heart. All of our prayers have one focus-His kingdom revealed. The makeup of our prayers is full of worship and thankfulness. Because of what He has done, He is our Lord, and we establish His supremacy and our loyalty to His will. This is our token of worship and thankfulness. His will has our allegiance and when we ask according to His will, we have what we ask.

PRAYER IN ACTION

"They came to a place named Gethsemane, and He said to His disciples, "Sit here until I have prayed." And He took with Him Peter and James and John and began to be very distressed and troubled. And He said to them, 'My soul is deeply grieved to the point of death; remain here and keep watch.' And He went a little beyond them, and fell to the ground and began to pray that if it were possible, the hour might pass Him by. And He was saying, 'Abba! Father! All things are possible for You; remove this cup from ME; yet not what I will, but what You will.' And He came and found them sleeping, and said to Peter, 'Simon, are you asleep? Could you not keep watch for one hour? Keep

watching and praying that you may not come into temptation; the spirit is willing, but the flesh is weak.'" Mark 14:32-38 (NASB)

Notice who Jesus brought with Him to prayer. The inner circle we have with us is just as important as the words that are prayed. Prayer is where you establish your agreement with God. In that regard, having those who agree with you can mean all the difference. There are moments in Jesus' earthly ministry when He removed people from the room. This was done because they didn't carry His same mind. **"For where two or three have gathered together in My name, I am there in their midst."** (Matthew 18:20, NASB).

Agreement is everything in prayer. Look at what happened at Pentecost. **"When the day of Pentecost had come, they were all together in one place."** (Acts 2:1, NASB). Their unity was the stage for Holy Spirit to be released. Power is unleashed within unity. Notice what Paul said to the Church in Philippi, **"make my joy complete by being of the same mind, maintaining the same love, united in spirit, intent on one purpose."** (Philippians 2:2, NASB). Agreement and unity are important in prayer.

Looking back at Mark 14, notice the people whom Jesus brought to the garden didn't join Him in prayer. This speaks of another aspect. You must pick your prayer partners wisely. The people you bring with you should help you, not hinder you. Jesus was the leader of this prayer meeting. Even though He trusted those He brought with Him, their lack of prayer didn't stop Him from praying effectively. No one should carry enough importance that they prevent you from partnering with your God concerning your situation. It's up to you, not them.

Next, look at what Jesus said in His prayer; **"yet not what I will, but what You will."** (Mark 14:36, NASB). This is one of the few moments we have in which a prayer of Christ is recorded and the focus of it is the Lordship of the Father. Since prayer is about establishing our partnership with God, I believe this is a crucial aspect.

And one last thing. Look at what Jesus told Peter when He caught him sleeping, "**Keep watching and praying that you may not come into temptation; the spirit is willing, but the flesh is weak.**" **(Mark 14:38, NASB)**. While Jesus was praying, Peter was sleeping. What Jesus warned him about is the fact that if he didn't pray, temptation would have more fighting power than normal. If you follow the story, you find out that Peter ended up denying Christ three times. It is my conviction, that if Peter had prayed with Christ before, He wouldn't have denied Christ later. If you pray before, you will be more prepared later. Your agreement in prayer will strengthen your allegiance in practice.

Let's summarize what we learned from Christ's example. When we pray with others, we must choose wisely who accompanies us. We understand that power falls on agreement, so we select those who are like-minded. Even though we all agree and trust one another, their absence doesn't hinder me. I receive their help, but God is my Father. Having prayer partners is not a requirement for approaching Him. Lastly, prayer weakens my flesh and hinders its influence in my life.

PRAYER RESULTS

We have seen Jesus instruct on prayer and we have seen a small moment in which He practiced prayer. Now, let's look at the results of His devotion to prayer.

"Therefore, Jesus answered and was saying to them, 'Truly, truly, I say to you, the Son can do nothing of Himself, unless it is something He sees the Father doing; for whatever the Father does, these things the Son also does in like manner. For the Father loves the Son, and shows Him all things that He Himself is doing; and the Father will show Him greater works than these, so that you will marvel.'" John 5:19-20 (NASB)

Prayer is the planning stage of your partnership with God. It is where He discusses His plans with you. If you don't enter a time of prayer, your communication with Him is limited, therefore, your partnership is hindered.

Remember, He partners with us to teach us˗to help us learn about Him and His ways˗for us to believe Him and ultimately become like Him. All of this is strengthened and secured when we dialogue with Him and learn more and more about Him. Christ was successful in all His endeavors because He knew how to cooperate with His Father to the degree that He acted and responded like His Father. He lived as the person He knew because He spent time with Him. He knew God's ways, so when His partner told Him "the way," He recognized it as such.

When Jesus said, **"He who has seen Me has seen the Father,"** **(John 14:9, NASB)**, it was more daring than we might think. Ponder this: Here was a man that was confident not only in His relationship with God, but in His ability to replicate God in the earth to the point that He didn't hesitate to announce, "When you see Me, you see the Father." I know it is easy to allow Christ's Godhood to give Him a pass. I agree. But remember, He lived life like we are supposed to˗as a man. How can He be an example to us, if He didn't live the life, we live?

Here was a man full of confidence in His relationship with His Father, as well as the demonstration of that relationship. Where do you think He received that confidence? -through prayer. He learned who His Father was, believed it, partnered with it, and became it˗which was made possible through prayer.

Notice in verse 20, it mentions how the Father shows the Son all things. Where do we think this occurs? -in prayer. "All things" means the knowledge of when something is coming; a warning about something; or a warning for someone; directives on conversing with a particular person; maybe instructions to avoid a person or to be patient with an individual. It is in prayer, where God reveals the steps of His plan˗how He plans on delivering what He's planning for you. Because you know Him, you believe Him when He directs you into position.

So yes, prayer is where we learn about Him which causes us to be like Him. This will make it easier to partner with Him. Jesus was so good at partnering with God because He knew Him so well. The more you know your partner, the easier it is to cooperate with Him. Since we know Him, we trust Him when He says specific things that are pivotal to the receiving of what He is giving. Through prayer, He positions us to receive what He is giving.

What is prayer? -an invitation to learn His heart. When His heart is uncovered, trust is born, leading us into a loving allegiance. But when we pray, we are not the only ones doing the talking. We value the opinion and wisdom of our covenantal partner. We listen more than we speak. Why? -because His words change us. Transformation happens not because of our words, but because of His. Here's another angle on this: If we give God more space to speak to us in prayer, we will then gain His viewpoint within a situation. The more He speaks, the more we listen-receiving and accepting that which is being said. The more we hear it, the more we will come to believe it, and when we believe it, we will do it. And remember, what happens when we do what we believe? -we see what we believe.

Prayer is communication between God and you, but unlike a simple earthly dialogue, prayer is a birthing place for transformation. Great wisdom and knowledge are passed to us from all moments of time. When we submit to them, the miraculous is achievable.

Grace gives, belief supports what is given, hope transports what is given, faith receives what is given, and prayer enlightens me on how to partner with what is given. Remember He is the Author of my faith, the Writer of my faith story. It is in prayer where He reveals to me the narrative.

Chapter 8: Opposition

SUMMARY

The entire process has now been covered. We ventured through three of the main covenants in the scriptures, understanding that covenant is how God defines His partnership. We saw how the Abrahamic covenant was an agreement between God, Abraham, and Abraham's descendants to possess the land-and all the blessings God offered. We learned that to keep the covenant, Abraham and those who followed had to be circumcised. Circumcision was their role and God was the Blesser. It was a covenant established upon belief.

Under the Old Covenant, we learned that Israel wanted to do things without God, removing Him from the role of the Initiator to the Observer. For Israel to be blessed, they had to keep the Law, which was impossible to obey because of their fallen nature. This caused them to always do that which God hates. They might keep one rule, but in disobeying even one, they were guilty of the whole thing. Being blessed was contingent on their obedience. They had to do good first, for God to bless them second. But God, rich in mercy, desired to manifest His love to His people. He instituted the sacrifices, a loophole of sorts, in which the death of an animal would take the penalty of the disobedience. Now, free from the consequence of their actions, God was able to bless them.

Under the New Covenant, we learned that Jesus did what no Israelite was able to do-keep the entire Law. He did what we couldn't do on our own. He became our spotless and perfect lamb. On the cross, He died in our place and took the penalty of our sins upon Himself, liberating us from death. We can now choose to do God's will instead of being forced to disobey. Christ's resurrection not only showed His victory over death, but it enabled Him to be the Negotiator and our Representative of the New Covenant.

Because He is our Representative in the covenant, the responsibility of the legalities within the covenant falls upon Him. When we receive Him, we receive His perfection. When God looks at us, He sees Christ's perfection, not our imperfection. Christ is the Possessor of all that we could ask or need, and because we are in Christ, we have access to it all. His life has become our life. His perfection has become our perfection. He is what we have become. In Christ, God declared that He will never allow our actions to dictate His again, but whether we see His blessings would be up to us. How do we receive all that God has given in Christ? -through faith or partnership with the Giver.

We learned about the Process of Faith. How we receive from God. How we partner with God. We learned how grace is the Giver and the beginning of the process. We start with grace because grace is God's part and His role. Grace is how He sees us and desires to work alongside us. When we step into partnership to receive from God, we start with Him and His viewpoint of us-and the fact that He has given us all things. This awareness is what influences our actions.

We saw how grace and Christ are connected, therefore, placing Christ at the forefront of all we do. He is our example and our source in everything we need to accomplish. He is our victory and because He is victorious-we are victorious. The message of grace in Christ is that God has given all things to us in Christ because of Christ in us.

We understand now that what we believe determines what we receive. Grace is the supporter of all that God wants to give to us and it assures that which God is giving gets to the believer. We understand that belief is birthed in the heart through what we hear consistently. What I hear over and over, I will come to believe. Belief moves me into action because I will always do what I believe. When I do what I believe, I become what I believe.

As we begin to receive, we start "in hope." We hold all God gives "in hope." We know His character and His ways-knowing He isn't a liar and what He has promised will come to pass. "In hope," we are looking for that which was promised in the natural. We confidently expect the promise to come while waiting patiently for its arrival.

Through faith, my belief shifts. I no longer believe the promise is coming, I now believe that the promise has arrived. It has always existed, in Christ, in the realm of the unseen. What was promised, was always mine in Christ. It has now become real to me, and no one can convince me that I don't have what God has given. I am fully persuaded just like Abraham before me. My belief moves me into partnering with what I believe through my words or any other action. When I do what I believe, faith is released, making what is true in the Heavenly realm manifest in the earth.

In prayer, God invites me to become like Him through revelation and communication. When I pray, His ways are revealed, which in turn, creates trust and transformation. Through my relationship with Him, I continue to become what I already am-like Him. The more like Him I become, the easier it becomes to partner with Him. He can speak to me and guide me in multiple ways that are familiar because I'm familiar with Him. Because I trust Him, I respond to His plan that positions me to receive what He has given.

In bringing all of this to a conclusion, we need to address the fact that each component in the Process of Faith has an opponent-something that the enemy uses to combat the working of the partnership. If the enemy can thwart any part, he can hinder us from receiving, and therefore prevent full partnership. God's will is only released in the earth through His partnership with us. If the enemy can stop that, he can stop the manifestation of God's will.

ENEMY OF GRACE

If you recall, at the transition from the Abrahamic Covenant to the Old, the Israelites wanted to do things on their own. God wanted to work with them, but Israel believed they could do all that God wanted without His help. This is the primary enemy of grace: our own self-effort.

"I have been crucified with Christ; and it is no longer I who live, but Christ lives in me; and the life which I now live in the flesh I live by faith in the Son of God, who loved me and gave Himself up for me. I do not nullify the grace of God, for if righteousness comes through the Law, then Christ died needlessly."
Galatians 2:20-21 (NASB)

Beginning with verse 20, we see a summary of sorts concerning all we have discussed. Christ is my example and my life. His ability is my ability. He is working through me as I cooperate with Him. The point of this verse is to show that Christ is my helper-the person in whom I depend. The opposite of that, would be me doing things on my own-refusing God's help while being in disobedience to Him and His ways. In this, I'm not yielded, I'm taking the lead.

Verse 21 teaches that Paul is aware of not nullifying the grace of God in his life. How could he nullify grace or prevent its operation in his life? -through self-effort, by depending on himself instead of God. Look at the last part of verse 21. Notice what is opposed to grace working in our lives. If righteousness, or right standing and acceptance by God, came through the Law, then Christ wouldn't have needed to die. Righteousness is the ability to stand before a holy God as if you have never sinned. Because I'm in Christ, and Christ is perfect and accepted by God, I'm in the same boat. All of this wasn't granted through obedience to the Law, but through faith in Christ.

If I could be accepted by God through my efforts alone, then Christ didn't need to come. To say I can do it on my own is to say Christ wasn't needed, and all the pain and suffering He bore on my account was worthless. We are basically slapping God in the face when we attempt to do things on our own.

So, what can help us with this? What can prevent us from depending on our self-effort. -honor. What you honor you attract. What you attract takes up your attention, and what has your attention has your allegiance.

In the Old Testament, there were moments in which the Israelites would make pillars or monuments at sites where God performed great works. These monuments served as reminders to the greatness of their God, and therefore what they would come to expect. They would tell stories to their children, thus carrying the greatness of God throughout the generations. The point is that these monuments represented what they honored. Notice these are the moments they thought important enough to remember in their culture. What they honored, they kept before them, thus assuring they didn't forget. What you don't forget has the potential to maintain influence.

So how do we put to death our self-effort? -by practicing honor. If we consistently honor what God has done, we attract and maintain the importance of what He has done in our lives. This maintains our allegiance. What you honor, you serve.

THE ENEMY OF OUR BELIEF

The enemy of belief is most likely obvious. Just as the opposite of grace is self-effort, the opposite of belief is unbelief.

"For we have become partaker of Christ, if we hold fast the beginning of our assurance firm until the end, while it is said, 'Today if you hear His voice, Do not harden your hearts, as when they provoked Me.' For who provoked Him when they had heard? Indeed, did not all those who came out of Egypt led my Moses? And with whom was He angry for forty years? Was it not with those who sinned, whose bodies fell in the wilderness? And to whom did He swear that they would not enter His rest, but to those who were disobedient? So, we see that they were not able to enter because of unbelief."
Hebrews 3:14-19 (NASB)

This reference summarizes what prevented Israel from going into the promised land. After the death of Moses, Joshua was to lead Israel into the land that was promised them through Abraham. Spies were sent to see the defenses they would need to address, and when they came back with their report, they sowed unbelief in the hearts of the people.

Remember, belief moves us into action. What I believe, will move me to partner through action. If I believe it, I will do it. So, if belief moves me, what does unbelief do? -it keeps me stuck. If belief moves me to partner with God, unbelief moves me to disconnect with God. What was God's will in the instance of the land? -It was their's to possess. All they had to do was partner with Him through belief. Joshua and Caleb said as much to the people.

"Joshua the son of Nun and Caleb the son of Jephunneh, of those who spied out the land, tore their clothes; and they spoke to all the congregation of the sons of Israel, saying. 'The land which we passed through to spy out is an exceedingly good land. If the LORD is pleased with us, then He will bring us into this land and give it to us- a land which flows with milk and honey. Only do not rebel against the LORD; and do not fear the people of the land, for they will be our prey. Their protection has been removed from them, and the LORD is with us; do not fear them.' But all the congregation said to stone them with stones. Then the glory of the LORD appeared in the tent of meeting to all the sons of Israel." **Numbers 14:6-10 (NASB)**

Look at the belief and the confidence of Joshua and Caleb. They believed in their God and were confident in their success to take that which God had promised. Because of their belief, they were moved to partner with God through their speech‑and if given the chance, their actions. Notice the unbelief of the people. Their unbelief kept them from possessing the land, and in fact, it led them into direct opposition to the will of God.

So, what does God do? -He allows them to stay in the wilderness until all the generations of those who didn't believe were dead. The only ones who remained were Joshua and Caleb‑those who partnered with God. Your unbelief will prevent partnership and thus possession of what God has given.

So, what is the solution to this issue? We technically have already covered this. To prevent unbelief, you must replace it with something you believe. How do we do that? -through the confession of God's word. Remember, confession is saying the same as someone else. If you are confessing the Word of God, you are constantly saying what God says. The more you speak, the more you hear. The more you hear, the more you believe. Speaking leads to believing.

This means that if you struggle to believe God in an arena, it's easily remedied. Just say what He says. If you say what He says, you will believe what He believes, and then you will do what He does.

THE ENEMY OF OUR HOPE

Remember that hope is a confident expectation. You are looking in the natural realm for what God has promised. The main thing to focus upon is that you're certain and fully persuaded that what was promised is coming. The opposite of true conviction is doubt.

Doubt defined by Websters means to be uncertain about something: to believe that something may not be true or is unlikely. Unbelief is being convinced something is false, while doubt is uncertainty. Sounds totally contrary to how God operates. Whether you're beginning "in hope," or have moved into faith, God still expects you to be fully convinced of His character. Who He is and how He operates is at the very core of our partnership with Him. Any element of doubt just hinders the process.

The real question that must be asked is what creates doubt? What sets the stage for you to be uncertain about a matter or situation? I would say it would be a lack of knowledge. Now you can argue that not knowing could lead to unbelief as well-but unbelief is certainty on the other side of the equation. You are certain about something with the knowledge you have now, and you have chosen not to believe. With doubt, you know you don't have all the facts; therefore, you are uncertain.

"My people are destroyed for lack of knowledge. Because you have rejected knowledge, I also will reject you from being My priest. Since you have forgotten the law of your God, I also will forget your children."
Hosea 4:6 (NASB)

Remember, this is Old Covenant so there are things you don't bring into your covenant. Just because you might reject something, doesn't mean He will reject you. Still, even though it's Old Covenant, that doesn't mean we get rid of it. What do we do when we are dealing with a different covenant? We don't replicate the actions. We replicate the heart behind it.

What is the message? -God tells the people that their lack of knowledge leads to destruction. What caused the lack of knowledge? -forgetting the Law. Let's take this and add it to what is said in the book of Joshua.

"This book of the law shall not depart from your mouth, but you shall meditate on it day and night, so that you may be careful to do according to all that is written; for then you will make your way prosperous, and then you will have success." Joshua 1:8 (NASB)

What led to success? -doing the Law. What led to doing the Law? -keeping the Law before them day and night. Remember, we aren't trying to be a success in the New Covenant. We aren't trying to be prosperous. We already are prosperous because of Christ. We aren't trying. We are partnering with what God has already said. How do we do that? -by keeping what He says before us day and night. Through meditating on His promises and confession, we will come to believe, then we will do, then we will become and see it all come to fruition. Here, we find the same result, but the motivation and opening response is different.

What creates doubt? -a lack of knowledge. What creates the lack of knowledge? -forgetting that which you once remembered. If you keep the truth of His Word before you day and night, you won't forget what God has said. Because you remember, you will be certain about His promises.

In closing, I want to strongly address something. There can be an attempt in our self-effort to do all that it takes to ensure we remember what we can. Not only can you not remember everything, but it's a weighted life trying to remember everything God wants you to learn.

Here's the thing. We deal in seeds, not always trees. When you learn something, your trust isn't in your ability to remember, but in His ability to remind you. **"But the Helper, the Holy Spirit, whom the Father will send in My name, He will teach you all things, and bring to your remembrance all that I said to you." (John 14:26, NASB).** Receive the seeds He is giving and, with His help, that knowledge will become the tree it's destined to be. Then go on to the next thing He is teaching. If you come across a situation that requires an old lesson, He will bring it back to you. Trust Him in all things!

THE ENEMY OF OUR FAITH

What is faith? Faith is the spiritual force that is released when we do what we believe. It is designed by God to bridge what is true in the Spirit to what needs to be true in the natural. We believe we have it in Christ, in the realm of the unseen. When we believe it, we act like what we believe is true. If I believe I'm prosperous in Christ, I will give generously according to what God wants me to give. I'm living out of the reality I believe to be true in the spiritual realm. When I do this, faith causes what is true in the spiritual to manifest in the natural. I don't live according to what I see in the natural, I live according to what I see in the spiritual. I live according to my faith, **"for we walk by faith, not by sight." (2 Corinthians 5:7, NASB).**

Now this is what we need to understand. Some people think that according to this verse, the enemy of our faith is sight, or what we see in the natural realm. That's not true. Yes, what we see in the natural can influence us, but it will only influence us if we allow it to do so. Faith doesn't ignore what is happening in the natural. It just doesn't give it a place of influence. You're choosing to believe what is true in the spiritual.

So, if sight isn't the enemy of faith, what is? Faith is the spiritual force God created for us to partner with Him. Fear is a demon that causes you partner with the devil. **"For God hath not given us the spirit of fear; but of power, and of love, and of a sound mind." (2 Timothy 1:7, KJV).** Fear doesn't necessarily stop you from operating in faith, but what it does is give you another option. Think about it. Faith is one of the leading elements in partnering with God. If the enemy wanted to prevent that, what better tactic could he tempt you with but to partner with him? If you partner with the devil, you can't partner with God.

Faith is created when you believe what God says and you step into action to partner with Him. Fear shows up when you believe what the devil says and you step into action to partner with him. Fear constantly tries to get your attention so that you believe the enemy's lies about the subject.

What's the solution? It all hinges on what you believe. To help in this vein we go back to our question, "How do we change what we believe?" If you have a problem with fear you believe the devil more than God. If you change what you believe, then you change with whom you partner. To change what you believe, you change what you have been speaking and to whom. What you say, you hear. What you hear and hear again, you will come to believe. To partner with God, believe God. To partner with the devil, believe the devil. The choice is yours.

THE ENEMY OF PRAYER

Prayer is communication with God. This is where we learn who He is and from where He reveals His wisdom and knowledge in any given situation. This develops trust in the carrying out of His plan. God speaks to us, and because we trust

Him and know Him, we listen and obey. This ultimately positions us to receive what God is giving. So, what is the enemy of prayer? Let's go back to Peter in the garden.

"Keep watching and praying that you may not come into temptation; the spirit is willing, but the flesh is weak." Mark 14:38 (NASB)

Jesus says the enemy of prayer is our flesh. There should be moments in our day set aside for prayer time. We all have had moments when the drive to pray just isn't there. It's these moments when our flesh has risen to offer its opinion. Whether we submit to it determines whether we carry out our prayer time or not. So, what is the remedy?

"But I say, walk by the Spirit, and you will not carry out the desire of the flesh. For the flesh sets its desire against the Spirit, and the Spirit against the flesh; for these are in opposition to one another, so that you may not do the things that you please." Galatians 5:16-17 (NASB)

Later in this chapter, Paul makes a list of things that the flesh desires, such as drunkenness and envying. However, the obvious fleshly desires that we call sin are not the only issue. The actions of the flesh include anything in direct opposition to the will of God. So, what is the solution to the issue?

"Now those who belong to Christ Jesus have crucified the flesh with its passions and desires. If we live by the Spirit, let us also walk by the Spirit." Galatians 5:24-25 (NASB)

Let's focus on verse 25 for the moment. What we see are two levels of spirituality-living and walking. The living will strengthen the walking. If we live by the Spirit, let us walk by the Spirit. What this verse is saying is what I've detailed throughout this book. We are not trying to become, we are living out of who we are, who God has called us to be.

What has God said about us in this instance? Look at verse 24. We have crucified the flesh and because we have done this through Christ, we live accordingly. Still, even though that is the reality we choose to believe and therefore live from- it's not always the reality that presents itself. So, what's the key? -we walk. We take every day that comes, choosing to live from the reality of what God says is true. As we believe it, we do it, and it will eventually show up. We have crucified the flesh, but we must continue to crucify the flesh in obedience to His truth abut us.

In all of this, we have talked about the Process of Faith and now we have talked about the enemies of that process-the enemies that would hinder you from partnering with God. In the next chapter, we will address what strong faith-a strong partnership-looks like. Why? -because a strong partnership can handle anything.

Chapter 9: Sin–the Enemy of the Process

INTRODUCTION

Sin is a familiar topic for every Christian. The Church culture you grew up in, or came out of, determines your viewpoint on the concept. Does the idea of sin bring fear, guilt, shame, condemnation, or uncertainty? Whatever the view, the knowledge of sin has always been present, and sadly, our understanding of the topic often determines our Christian progress.

Remember we are discussing the Process of Faith and how to partner with God. Truly, one of the greatest hindrances to the entire process, and not just its specific components, would be the concept of sin. When talking about partnership, communication and fellowship are key components to a successful cooperation with God. But as we discovered in Genesis, when sin arrived on the scene, separation and isolation were the end result. In a covenant of grace, we have been set free from the bondage of sin because of what Christ did upon the cross. Still, this defeated foe has often been allowed to pollute those liberated as if they had never left the prison. Let's take the time to venture into this and see how sin hinders our faith, and as a result, our partnership with God.

IN THE BEGINNING

Let's begin by looking at how sin came into being. First, we need to set the tone. In the beginning, God created the heavens and the earth. Genesis chapter 1 explains the process and what was created each day. At the end of each day, and at the end of each major moment of creating, God looked at what He created and announce that it was good. Moving forward into day 6, God created Adam, in other words humanity. He blessed Adam and at the conclusion of the day, again God looked at what He created, which included Adam, and said that it was very good.

Now let's look at things a little closer. What we are about to witness is the creation of humanity. If we take a close look at the happenings that are occurring, we will see why we were created in the first place. Chapter 1 is about creation week-the specific days in which God created the earth. Chapter 2 is the explanation of how God finished His work, and then rested.

"Thus the heavens and the earth were completed, and all their hosts. By the seventh day God completed His work which He had done, and He rested on the seventh day from all His work which He had done. Then God blessed the seventh day and sanctified it, because in it He rested from His work which God had created and made. This is the account of the heavens and the earth when they were created, in the day that the Lord God made earth and heaven."
Genesis 2:1-4 (NASB)

As we can see, in verses 1 through 4, God finished creation and then rested. He was finished, done, and everything was complete. Now look at verse 5:

"Now no shrub of the field was yet in the earth, and no plant of the field had yet sprouted, for the LORD God had not sent rain upon the earth, and there was no man to cultivate the ground." **Genesis 2:5 (NASB)**

Here's the point I want to make: God had already created humanity. We see that in verses 2 and 3; then He rested on the seventh day due to His work being finished. But now, in verse 5, there seems to be a reversal of sorts. It appears we have gone back in time to a point in which man hadn't yet been created. As we continue throughout the chapter, we see an in-depth description of the Garden of Eden and how it was created and watered.

"But a mist used to rise from the earth and water the whole surface of the ground. Then the LORD God formed man of dust from the ground, and breathed into his nostrils the breath of life; and man became a living being. The LORD God planted a garden toward the east, in Eden; and there He placed the man whom He had formed. Out of the ground the LORD God caused to grow every tree that is pleasing to the sight and good for food; the tree of life also in the midst of the garden, and the tree of the knowledge of good and evil. Now a river flowed out of Eden to water the garden; and from there it divided and became four rivers The name of the first is Pishon; it flows around the whole land of Havilah, where there is gold. The gold of that land is good; the bdellium and the onyx stone are there. The name of the second river is Gihon; it flows around the whole land of Cush. The name of the third river is Tigris; it flows east of Assyria. And the fourth river is the Euphrates. Then the LORD God took the man and put him into the garden of Eden to cultivate it and keep it."
Genesis 2:6-15 (NASB)

What has happened is the author of the book of Genesis has taken us back to day six and keys in on the events of that day. Chapter 1 and the first four verses of chapter 2 are an overview of the creation week. But the rest of chapter 2 is an in-depth look at day six in which "**God saw all that He had made, and behold, it was very good." (Genesis 1:31, NASB)**. What was so important about day six? It was where humanity came onto the scene.

I want to submit to you that the events of day six are man focused. What I mean by that is that everything God does on this day is specifically with humanity in mind. What is so important about day six? -it shows us the whole point to creation in the first place. Everything that was created from day one to day six was for humanity. God didn't just create a planet, then place mankind on it to keep it so He could sit back. No, God created a place worthy enough for the greatness He was about to establish, the presence of His beloved.

THE TRUTH ABOUT HUMANITY

Let's look at the events of day six in sequential order. When we look at the order in which things were created, we see something interesting about the nature of our existence.

The following events are in chronological order according to verses 6 through 15 of chapter 2:

- A mist comes up from the ground to water the ground (vs. 6)
- God forms man and man becomes alive (vs. 7
- God plants a garden in Eden (vs. 8)
- God places the man He created at the place in which the garden was planted (vs. 8)
- God brings forth trees and other plants that were pleasing to the eye and for food (vs.9)
- God plants the Tree of Life and the Tree of the Knowledge of Good and Evil in the middle of the garden (vs. 9)
- A river comes out of Eden, forms four rivers and branches out to water the garden (vs. 10)

- A description is recorded of the four rivers and the lands in which they watered (vs. 11-14)
- Man is placed within the garden to cultivate it and keep it (vs. 15)

Take a closer look at the order of events within chapter 2 and pay careful attention to where man falls within all of this. I want to show you how the important details of this list really pinpoint the truth that humanity was God's focus. Let's start with where it talks about the mist covering the ground.

"But a mist used to rise form the earth and water the whole surface of the ground." **Genesis 2:6 (NASB)**

When we take the time to look up the words mist and water in the original language, we get a picture easily missed when just reading through Genesis. The word mist gives us the sense of enveloping. Basically, this mist covered the entire ground; no piece of the ground was missed. The word water means "to give drink." To put it into greater context, that word is also translated as "cupbearer." A cupbearer's job was to be the possessor of the cup from which the king would drink. It was a place of honor as well as affording protection due to the possibility of the king being poisoned. It was a position of trust and familiarity with the king.

Keep the honorable and trusting position of the cupbearer in your mind as you imagine a mist watering the ground. The scene set before you shouldn't just invoke images of watering the ground like you would in your backyard. The tone is more sacred. When a king had a designated cupbearer, he didn't take a drink from just any cup, from just any person. This mist in Genesis 1:6 was chosen for this task.

You might be thinking, "Nathan it's just a mist!" Maybe, but sometimes we need to sit back and let God tell His own story. What is the story? -the setup for His masterpiece. When I've read this verse before, it never really had any major impact. I understood that the rains hadn't come yet because Noah and the flood story had yet to happen. To me it was just a method chosen by God to water the grounds for the plants to come forth. But did you notice that in verse 7, the verse right after the watering of the ground, plants are not what is mentioned? What happens in verse 7? -the forming of man.

"Then the LORD God formed man of dust from the ground, and breathed into his nostrils the breath of life; and man became a living being."
Genesis 2:7 (NASB)

Adam's creation is depicted in the word "formed." The word used means to form, fashion, and frame. The sense is a potter framing and molding clay into the desired form. Go back to that trusting and protecting scene that was represented by the watering of the ground. It's this picture where man is created. A king chooses his cupbearer. A potter chooses his clay. God set the stage for the creation of mankind. There are no words in the English language at my disposal to convey the emotion I felt when the Lord explained this to me. I want to encourage you to stop reading at this moment and allow the Holy Spirit to minister to you the emotions and the imaginings of your Heavenly Father as He was forming Adam: The love and adoration for this person; the fact that He trusted him; and the fact that He desired to protect and comfort him. Now take that feeling and allow the Holy Spirit to point it at you. You weren't just created; you were formed. Your life wasn't a mistake or just a combination of circumstances. God took years of time to form you before your momentous arrival. You are beautiful to Him, and you always will be.

The watering of the ground wasn't just so that plants could spring up! It was God setting up the environment in which

134

He was going to bestow the ultimate devotion of His love, the supreme possessor of His affections and devotion-humanity.

After Adam was formed, verse 8 tells us that God planted a garden and placed Adam in the land in which the garden was planted. Now here's the thing I want you to hone in on. Notice that plants and trees started springing up in verse 9 after Adam was placed there. What this tells me is that the garden wasn't visible yet when it was planted in verse 8. It couldn't have been if trees started sprouting up in verse 9. So, with this train of thought, God planted the garden, placed Adam upon the land from which the garden is about to spring forth, and then allowed the garden to form before Adam's eyes. It says in verse 9 that God caused the trees to grow. They didn't just pop into existence. They grew and matured before Adam. Can you imagine the awe Adam experienced when he witnessed actual creation. Not only did Adam see the trees, but he saw the rivers form and begin to flow. God was literally performing wonders before Adam. God was introducing Himself to His beloved. After God created the garden, in verse 15, the NASB says Adam was "put into" the garden. In verse 8, Adam was "placed," but in verse 15, he was "put into." There is a different picture here in verse 15 in comparison to verse 8. Adam was placed or positioned previously. Why? -so he would be perfectly located to see creation. Imagine a joyful and excited God actually taking the time to put Adam in the perfect spot to see His wonders. Then after His wonders were completed, He brings Adam into it for an up-close tour of all that God was giving to him.

You might be thinking that this is so contrary to the picture of God with which you are acquainted. Is this so far off the mark in knowing the character of the Creator with which you are familiar? What does a creator do? -they create. What does a creator do after they create? -they show off what they made. This is exactly what God is doing. He is performing creation in the presence of His ultimate creation-and He's having the time of His life doing it!

I have taken the time to go into detail concerning the sixth day to show you the truth concerning our existence. Did you notice throughout this entire chapter, nothing was described, explained, or presented to give you the idea that Adam did anything for God? Let's make it even more clear. Look at chapter 1 verses 26 through 30. We have seen God's actions in the creation of mankind, but now let's hear His intentions for mankind from His very mouth.

> *"Then God said, 'Let Us make man in Our image, according to Our likeness; and let them rule over the fish of the sea and over the birds of the sky and over the cattle and over all the earth, and over every creeping thing that creeps on the earth.' God created man in His own image, in the image of God He created him; male and female He created them. God blessed them; and God said to them, "Be fruitful and multiply, and fill the earth, and subdue it; and rule over the fish of the sea and over the birds of the sky and over every living thing that move on the earth.' Then God said, "Behold, I have given you every plant yielding seed that is on the surface of all the earth, and every tree which has fruit yielding seed; it shall be food for you; and to every beast of the earth and to every bird of the sky and to every thing that moves on the earth which has life, I have given every green plant for food'; and it was so."*
> **Genesis 1:26-30 (NASB)**

Verse 26 is God declaring His intentions for mankind. The verse is split into two ideas: identity and application. The identity piece is man being formed in the image and likeness of God. The application piece is the rulership of man over the earth. Notice which came first. God intended to instill identity before authority. He wants us to know who we are before He gives us something to do. Often, we are begging and crying out to the Lord to tell us what we are supposed to be doing when He is trying to tell you who you are. Instead of trying to figure out what to do, let God tell you who you are, and through the journey of self-discovery (which is found in Him), you will find your purpose.

Verse 27 is God forming mankind, both male and female. Verse 28 is the declaration of the blessing. God wasn't conversing with Adam and Eve. He was speaking over them. He is creating and establishing the very nature and mindset of the pair through His words.

Up to this point, God has either spoken to Himself, or made declarations into Adam and Eve. The first words Adam and Eve heard framed their identity. Verse 29 is the application of that identity. Now in verse 26, we know that the application piece involves rulership over the earth but notice that isn't what God tells them in verse 29. He doesn't say, "This is what I want you to do." He tells them this is what He has done. And what has He done? -He has given!!!!

If you could have only seen the excitement I had when I saw this for the first time. Even here at the origin of mankind, we see the beginning of the Process of Faith-the beginning of partnership. God's loving nature expressed through giving has always been at the origin of all things, and we see it here for humanity. If the importance of God giving to us is highlighted at the beginning of our formation, how much more should we be dependent upon His giving now? What He has done is the very foundation of our existence. He gave us life and He has been giving ever since.

This is where religion pokes its ugly head. Who has heard this statement? - "I was created to worship Him." Nowhere in these verses that speak about the establishment of the human race do we see anything about what humans were to be doing for God. The entire creation story isn't about what we could do for Him, but rather what He could, and is doing for us. As I write this, I sense the possible hesitation from some who might be reading. It has been ingrained within us that we need to do great things for God, but God never said anything like that to Adam and Eve. Look at it: nowhere in Genesis chapters 1 and 2 do we see any conversation between man and God in which

God tells them what to do. All we see is God doing and eventually explaining what He has done. Now there is one moment in which God gives instruction but before we look at that, follow me here. I want you to understand that it wasn't Adam's activity God focused upon, but his being. Adam wasn't made to do but rather to be‑and out of that being, he was to do.

I was not created to love God. I was created to be loved by Him. We have done an excellent job at shifting the focus of the Gospel towards God when the whole story of the Bible has been towards us. We find this hard to accept because we have adopted this identity of inferiority when it comes to the things of God. We have allowed the enemy to bring shame and a false sense of humility, which is really a form of control and abasement. Do you want to know why Adam and Eve didn't have a problem with feeling inferior before God? Because all they knew was that God was for them, and that He loved them, and that He was always devoted to them. God's love for them was the only reality they were acquainted with, and it was that reality from which they lived. What would we be able to achieve on this side of the cross, empowered by and through the Holy Spirit, if we learned to do this‑to live out of His reality and not the one that is presented before us in this natural world? It's possible, but only through faith‑through partnership.

Now you might be thinking, "So Adam did nothing? He just spent his whole life being loved by God?" Well, if you read chapter 2, you know that wasn't the case.

"Out of the ground the LORD God formed every beast of the field and every bird of the sky, and brought them to the man to see what he would call them; and whatever the man called a living creature, that was its name."
Genesis 2:19 (NASB)

So, what did Adam do? -the exact thing that God performed for him. What did God do when Adam was formed?

138

He proclaimed identity over him and into him. And not just any identity, but God's own identity. Because of this, when Adam was given animals, He named them. By naming them, he gave them identity. How did Adam know to do this? We are never given any communication between God and Adam in which he learned what needed to be done. But it is safe to say that Adam did what he saw God do. Does this sound familiar?

"Therefore, Jesus answered and was saying to them, 'Truly truly, I say to you, the Son can do nothing of Himself, unless it is something He sees the Father doing; for whatever the Father does, these things the Son also does in like manner." John 5:19 (NASB)

Notice how Christ mirrors what He sees His Father do. This is the same tactic that Adam used in the garden. There is no instruction, no explanation, Adam simply operated out of identity-the identity that was sown into him at formation. Adam received what was given to him by God and then did what He saw God do with what he had been given. This is partnership at its finest. This is the thing for which we were crafted. Not simply to love God with all our heart, but to know that this desire is only an expression of what you have received-the unconditional love of your Father. We were crafted to receive and then partner with God in the operation of what we receive.

Therefore, faith is so important! Faith is the force God has set up for us to receive from Him. When we receive from Him-when we receive what Grace has made available-we then partner with Him, not only to bring it into the natural, to see it with our own eyes, but to also direct it and channel it into the world. You can't give what you haven't first received. Your activity in the world should always be a response to what you have received from the Lord. That was how partnership was done in the garden, and it is the same today!

SEPARATION

We have now established the tone of the garden. We saw how God passionately formed man, then introduced and expressed Himself to His beloved through what He gave. We then saw Adam take that which he received and replicate it in the garden. Adam did what he saw God do. It was a perfect existence filled with communion and liberty. But Genesis chapter 3 changed everything.

In Genesis 2:16, we see God giving a command to Adam concerning the Tree of the Knowledge of Good and Evil.

"The LORD God commanded the man saying, 'From any tree of the garden you may eat freely; but from the tree of the knowledge of good and evil you shall not eat, for in the day that you eat from it you will surely die.'"
Genesis 2:16-17 (NASB)

Now herein lies the situation in which we find Adam. Up to this point, he lived his entire existence knowing nothing but God's love. Everywhere he looked, he saw the trees, the animals and all the things that God created and then gave to him. He walked in the cool of the day, always talking and communing with God. The presence of God was continually present in Adam's life.

When we talk about a partnership, or a relationship, there are always at least two parties involved. For the relationship to be healthy, both participants must choose the other. Remember God isn't a dictator. He's a gracious, kind, lover of people. Yes, God lavished His love unconditionally and without measure upon Adam, but God wouldn't force Adam to love Him back. As God chose Adam, Adam must choose God. God chose to partner with Adam, and for the partnership to be maintained, Adam needed to one thing. He needed to return the favor.

"Now the serpent was more crafty than any beast of the field which the LORD God had made. And he said to the woman, 'Indeed, Has God said, 'You shall not eat from any tree of the garden?' The woman said to the serpent, 'From the fruit of the trees of the garden we may eat; but from the fruit of the tree which is in the middle of the garden, God has said, 'You shall not eat from it or touch it, or you will die.'' The serpent said to the woman, 'You surely will not die! For God knows that in the day you eat from it your eyes will be opened, and you will be like God, knowing good and evil.' When the woman saw that the tree was good for food, and that it was a delight to the eyes, and that the tree was desirable to make one wise, she took from its fruit and ate; and she gave also to her husband with her, and he ate." Genesis 3:1-6 (NASB)

We have established that Adam was deeply familiar with the love of God. Again, everywhere he looked, Adam was reminded of God's giving nature. So, when the enemy came to tempt them, what did he attack? ‾the love of God; specifically, His giving nature. After the devil started the conversation with an opening question to Eve in verse 1, he then asked a second question designed to hit his target. This altercation reveals to us the chosen method of the enemy in how he brings temptation. And take note, he does it this way every time.

The first thing that the devil attacked was the Word of God. Every time the enemy tempts us, he always starts by sowing confusion into our foundation‾the Word of God. The devil knew the truth. To deceive someone, you must know the truth. If he could shake Adam and Eve's understanding of God's goodness in any measure, their stance would be less and less secure. So, understand this: if you find it hard to stand in faith concerning a matter, it's possible you might not fully understand God's love in that arena. **"For in Christ Jesus neither circumcision nor uncircumcision means anything, but faith working through love." (Galatians 5:6, NASB)**. If the love of God isn't known in an area, your ability to move in faith is hindered. Again, that is why we start with Grace because it's all about His love for us.

The second thing the devil did was shift their gaze. Every time you have chosen to sin, you chose it out of a lack of

141

understanding, or because God's Word wasn't clear or fully received. This caused your gaze to be moved from where God had placed it. Where was Adam and Eve's gaze consistently located? Where did God leave it?

"Then God said, 'Behold, I have given you every plant yielding seed that is on the surface of all the earth, and every tree which has fruit yielding seed; it shall be food for you.'" **Genesis 1:29 (NASB)**

Take the word behold. In that, God was saying, "look at this." In other words, God told them to look at what He had done and what He had already given. Now let me add something else to this: this statement in verse 29 also includes the Tree of the Knowledge of Good and Evil. At that moment, He didn't exclude the Tree of the Knowledge of Good and Evil. In fact, God never said He didn't give that tree to Adam. He told Adam not to eat of it. In other words, the Tree of the Knowledge of Good and Evil was rightfully given to Adam, but He was commanded not to eat of it. Picture it: Adam was tasked with cultivating and maintaining the garden. Since the Tree of the Knowledge of Good and Evil was a part of the garden, his task included that tree. When God told Adam and Eve not to eat of the tree, God was telling them what to do with something that belonged to them.

Everything on that planet belonged to Adam. Everything in that garden belonged to Adam. This also included the Tree of the Knowledge of Good and Evil. He had the free will to do whatever he saw fit in the Garden. The problem was, never had it entered Adam's mind to do something contrary to what God wanted. That was the true message of the enemy. "You have freedom. You don't have to do what God says." Was that true? -yes. Was it beneficial advice? -no! The moment Adam and Eve chose to do something their own way, their allegiance shifted from God to the devil, thus causing for the first time ever, a separation between humanity and God. This separation was the true definition of death. God told them this would happen if they ate of the tree. **"...but from the tree of the knowledge of good and evil you shall not eat, for in the day that you eat from it you will surely die."** **(Genesis 2:17, NASB).**

HEARTBROKEN

You probably find it interesting that most of this chapter is written about the goodness of God, and yet this is a chapter about sin. The reason for this is simple-when we talk about sin, we mainly focus on our actions and our choices. You can't talk about sin and take humanity out of the conversation. We were the ones who did it and still commit it. But we must understand that sin stole from God way more than it ever stole from us. We can't even grasp the full weight of the fall of mankind if we simply focus on what we've lost. We need to see that God lost His heart, His beloved, His compatriot, the one He loved.

Think about it: Adam and God were so united-they were never apart. They ate together. They conversed together. They walked together. We say that the most heartbreaking words in scripture are **"I never knew you; depart from Me, you who practice lawlessness."** **(Matthew 7:23, NASB).** But let me submit to you that the most heart wrenching words in scripture come from our God when He called out to Adam **"...where are you?"** **(Genesis 3:9, NASB).**

How dare us think that sin only affected us! I believe this thought alone could be one of the greatest lies of the enemy-the thought that God didn't come out of this unscathed. The fact of the matter is sin did and has always caused division. It took Adam one step in a different direction that created a chasm that took generations to fill back up.

The lesson of sin is this: it is the ultimate enemy to partnership. Whenever you sin, you have chosen to do things

143

your way, apart from God's opinions and desires. Every time we sin, we hurt God and deepen our separation from Him. Sin has always been, no matter what covenant you are under, a separator. It looks different under the New Covenant, but it's still the same result. Ask anyone who is a Christian who has a history of being trapped in sin. They will always tell you that the moments they weren't committing the sin is when they felt the closest to God. And they will tell you that sin deadened their heart towards the things of God. Why? Let's look back at Genesis.

"Then the eyes of both of them were opened, and they knew that they were naked; and they sewed fig leaves together and made themselves loin covering. They heard the sound of the LORD God walking in the garden in the cool of the day and the man and his wife hid themselves from the presence of the LORD God among the trees of the garden." **Genesis 3:7-8 (NASB)**

What happened right after Adam and Eve sinned? -they hid themselves from the Lord. This was the first sin committed by humanity and look at the result-they hid themselves. They pushed themselves away from the one person who loved them unconditionally. It's the same today. There is always something in us that wants to run from God whenever we mess up. The difference between us and Adam was that Adam had nowhere to run. Not only did sin push Adam apart from God, but it also kept God away. God is holy and what does holiness do to sin? -it burns it up. Therefore, under the Law in the Old Covenant, the High Priests had to tie ropes around their ankles before they went into the Holy of Holies where the presence of God dwelled. If they didn't perform the sacrifices correctly to cover their sins before they approached the holiness of God, they were instantly killed. God didn't kill them, but the very essence of His presence did. God stayed away to preserve them. Can you imagine loving someone so much that staying away was the only course of action to protect them. That my friends, is the tragedy of the Fall; that an all-compassionate God who created us to be loved up close, could only love us from afar.

But glory to God! Because of Christ, sin has been dealt with on the cross. There is no longer a barrier keeping God away from me. His very presence is the most soothing and comforting atmosphere in which we crave. His presence is always with us and is never kept from us.

Even though sin has been made powerless, it doesn't mean it's void of influence. When Adam sinned, he had no choice but to run away. But for us who have been delivered from the penalty of sin, we have a choice. **"For the wages of sin is death, but the free gift of God is eternal life in Christ Jesus our Lord." (Romans 6:23, NASB).** Whenever we sin, even though we have messed up, because of what Christ has done, we can **"draw near with confidence to the throne of grace, so that we may receive mercy and find grace to help in time of need." (Hebrews 4:16, NASB).** Sin has been made powerless. There is nothing preventing us from receiving all that God has for us, including and especially, God Himself. The veil has been torn in two. Nothing is stopping us from entering God's presence. Nothing except what you allow.

THE GRACE TRAP

In the closing of this chapter, I need to make something abundantly clear. When we talk about grace, we are referring to the barriers and limitations that have held us back-which have now been removed. The enemy has been defeated and we have been liberated, not because of what we have done, but because of Christ. It was His efforts that tipped the scale in our favor. His works that are the determining factor in why I'm blessed. I'm not saved/blessed because of what I have done, but because of what He has done. My salvation is not determined by my actions. The blood of Christ is far more powerful to work salvation for me than my actions are to "unsave" me. My salvation is secure because the blood of Christ is secure.

"The former priests, on the one hand, existed in greater numbers because they were prevented by death from continuing, but Jesus, on the other hand, because He continues forever, holds His priesthood permanently. Therefore, He is able also to save forever those who draw near to God through Him, since He always lives to make intercession for them. For it was fitting for us to have such a high priest, holy, innocent, undefiled, separated from sinners and exalted above the heavens; who does not need daily, like those high priests, to offer up sacrifices, first for His own sins and then for the sins of the people, because this He did once for all when He offered up Himself."
Hebrews 7:23-27 (NASB)

Because of what I have just said, I need to make this next statement clear. Sin has been dealt with forever through the offering of Christ as my substitute. But just because sin has been made powerless, this doesn't mean I am to continue in sin. Just because sin no longer stops me from being blessed, doesn't mean I allow its influence to remain. Paul was a grace teacher and at times, he had to confront the idea that just because I can do whatever I want and still go to Heaven, doesn't mean I should. Let's look at this:

"For if by the transgression of the one, death reigned through the one, much more those who receive the abundance of grace and of the gift of righteousness will reign in life through the One, Jesus Christ."
Romans 5:17 (NASB)

This verse makes it abundantly clear that my ability to reign in life is entirely based on the abundance of grace and the gift of righteousness, not on my ability to do right. To make this clearer, Paul talks about this entirely in chapter 6 of Romans.

146

"What shall we say then? Are we to continue in sin so that grace may increase?
May it never be! How shall we who died to sin still live in it?"
Romans 6:1-2 (NASB)

Paul makes it perfectly clear that through the cross of Jesus Christ, we have been made dead to sin. If we are dead to it, then why would we continue to live in sin? Because I'm dead to sin, sin has no hold over me. We can choose not to sin, "... **having been freed from sin, you became slaves of righteousness."** (**Romans 6:18, NASB).**

Now no matter how you slice it, there will always be people that will hear the message of grace and say that they are free to do whatever they want. They are totally correct in this. The problem is that even though God will still love them, if they continue to choose a life of sin, the death they have been liberated from will eventually ooze back into their life. What would happen if you slept with a corpse? You would get up smelling like death. It's the same concept. If you naturally wouldn't sleep with the dead, why would you spiritually partake of that to which you have died?

This is what is happening to those who continue to choose sin over the grace of God. If the grace of God is designed to empower you to quit sinning, and you keep choosing to sin, then you are consistently ignoring the power that has been made available to help you. What would happen if you continued to ignore God's help? Eventually, the influence grace has in your life would start to dwindle. Grace doesn't stop flowing. It will always be present, but if you decide not to partner with it through faith, you will no longer receive its benefits. It is the grace of God through faith that freed you from your old life. Without it, that old life would return. What happens after a length of time spent returning to your old life? That life will become your new life. You have then resurrected that which was killed. By

147

doing so, you become comfortable with the grave from which you were rescued.

So why is sin the enemy of our partnership with God? Because it is designed to cause division. Every time you choose sin, you choose yourself over Him. You choose your wisdom over His-your ability over His ability, your actions over His grace, your grave over His life. Separated partners can't cooperate with each other, and above all, can't benefit from one another. Since our part of the partnership greatly depends on His, a life of sin separates us from the very person and power needed to live rightly. Our partnership with God is the very thing that enables us to live this life to the measure in which He has destined. Living a life of sin-always choosing myself over Him-prevents me from experiencing the abundant life that Jesus came to give.

CHAPTER 10–THE NATURE OF FAITH

INTRODUCTION

At this point, as we start wrapping it up, I would like to cover a story in the Gospels that signifies an important concept about faith that has yet to be discussed. It also highlights other components in play, which is a good demonstration of the Process of Faith.

A LACK OF FAITH

"And when they were come to the multitude, there came to him a certain man, kneeling down to him, and saying, 'Lord, have mercy on my son: for he is a lunatic, and sore vexed: for ofttimes he falleth in the fire, and oft into the water. And I brought him to thy disciples, and they could not cure him.' Then Jesus answered and said, 'Oo faithless and perverse generation, how long shall I be with you? bring him hither to me.' And Jesus rebuked the devil; and he departed out him: and the child was cured from that very hour. Then came the disciples to Jesus apart, and said, 'Why could not we cast him out? And Jesus said unto them, Because of your unbelief: for verily I say unto you, If ye have

149

faith as a grain of mustard seed, ye shall say unto this mountain, Remove hence to yonder place; and it shall remove; and nothing shall be impossible unto you. Howbeit this kind goeth not out but by prayer and fasting.'"
Matthew 17:14-21 (KJV)

First things first-our questions. Because it is recorded under the Old Covenant. To whom is Jesus speaking? -His disciples. What was the question? -Why couldn't they cast the demon out of the boy. Because Jesus wasn't talking to the Pharisees but His disciples, this could be an indication that He wasn't talking about the Law. Also, the question had nothing to do with the Law or what they needed to do to earn something, but their question had to do with why they weren't successful in a given activity. So, we can conclude that what is described here is Jesus explaining a New Covenant concept.

Here's the situation. A father showed up asking Jesus to heal his son. The father said that the boy was possessed by a demon which caused him to fall into fire and water. He claimed that he went to the disciples, but they couldn't do anything. So, he asked for Jesus' help.

First, let's look at Jesus' response, **"O faithless and perverse generation, how long shall I be with you?" (Matthew 17:17, KJV)**. To whom is Jesus speaking? There are four people involved in these events-the father, the son, Christ, and the disciples. Christ wasn't talking to Himself, and He wasn't talking to the son since the boy was the victim. So, this leaves only the father and the disciples.

When we read this, we often conclude that Jesus is frustrated with the disciples because they couldn't cast the demon out. It's a logical conclusion and it's one I've had for many years, but it's not the correct one. Why? -because nowhere in the Gospels do we see Christ frustrated with the actions of people except for the Pharisees. If Jesus is irritated, it's because of their lack of faith.

We automatically assume He is frustrated with actions because that is what is visible, but most of the time Jesus doesn't comment on what they did, but rather the influence behind it. You did this because of your lack of faith. Remember, faith is supported by actions-no action, no faith. Faith is visible because actions are visible. What you do, determines whether you are "in faith" or not. Where do your actions come from? -what you believe. What you believe will move you into doing what you believe. If what you believe is in accordance with God and what He has said, then your actions create faith. Whenever Jesus mentions their lack of faith, it is because He understands that what they believe isn't in line with God's way of thinking, thus hindering them from partnership.

What do you think Jesus was referring to when He said, **"O faithless generation?"** What is a generation? -a group of people gathered based on when they were born. Generational groupings cover a multiple number of years, even decades. He didn't say faithless disciples or faithless man, He said faithless generation. I propose that Jesus wasn't irritated with just the disciples, but with the father as well. My reasoning is found in Jesus's answer to the disciples' question.

They asked why they couldn't cast the demon out. Jesus responded that it was because of their unbelief. Here is my question. Why were the disciples certain that they couldn't cast the demon out? -because they didn't see any change in the boy. They allowed what they saw with their natural eyes to determine what they believed. Because they saw no change, they believed there to be no change.

It's the same with the father. Because he saw no change, he believed that the disciples failed in their attempt. I think this might have been the first time that there wasn't an immediate change when the disciples operated in their authority. This was used by Christ to teach on the nature of faith. Therefore, I believe that Jesus was frustrated with both the father and the disciples because they allowed what they were witnessing with their eyes to determine what was true.

What should they have done? Look at what happened when Christ casts the demon out in verse 18. It says that the demon left immediately but the boy was cured later. In other words, the spirit left, but there was no physical evidence of the spirit's departure until a later time.

Here's my point. When Jesus rebuked the devil, He believed despite whatever physical evidence He saw before Him because He operated in authority. The moment He spoke, the devil had no choice but to leave. He wasn't looking for it in the natural like a person "in hope." It was a done deal to Him because of what He believed to be true in the Spirit, even though He had to wait to see it come to pass.

Maybe, when Jesus said the disciples couldn't do it because of their unbelief, He was saying to them, "If you really believed, what you experienced in the natural wouldn't have moved you." What were they to believe in? -the authority that Christ gave them earlier in Matthew chapter 10. Jesus gave them the authority to cast out devils, not part of the time, but every time. Just because it appeared to be taking longer didn't mean it wasn't working.

In Mark 11, Jesus cursed a fig tree that didn't have any figs. Nothing seemed to happen in the natural. The next day, the disciples were in awe when they saw the fig tree had died. Jesus wasn't in awe because He knew that the moment He cursed it, it happened-it was a done deal. That tree had no choice but to die. It's the same thing with us and everything we do in faith. If we really believe it, we wouldn't allow what happens in the natural to derail us from our stance of faith.

How many times have we gone to the healing line expecting an immediate manifestation and not received it? The truth is, you received it when you were born again. You received it when Christ became united with you. You received it when you said Jesus is the Lord of my Life. You received it when you were grafted into the vine. You received it then and you have it now. You went to that healing line not to get healed, not to see if God was going to heal you, but to partner with a like-minded believer in faith to bring about what was already true. If you don't see it naturally, you better see it spiritually. With the eyes of faith, I see myself whole and well. I see my family coming to Christ. I see my life with no lack enabling me to give liberally. I believe the truth, no matter what I see in the natural because I already have it in the spiritual. If I believe it, I will do it, and I will see it.

Jesus said they couldn't cast the demon out because of their unbelief. If they had believed, they wouldn't have allowed what appeared to be happening in the natural move them from their stance of faith. Sometimes, your faith isn't visible by what you say or give, but by your stubbornness to keep standing. I know what I believe, and I refuse to allow any situation, or any person remove me. God has done too much for me not to take Him at His Word. He said it and that settles it.

THE NATURE OF FAITH

Stay with me as I kill a religious calf by unpacking this well used verse.

"And Jesus said unto them, Because of your unbelief: for verily I say unto you, If ye have faith as a grain of mustard seed, ye shall say unto this mountain, Remove hence to yonder place; and it shall remove; and nothing shall be impossible unto you." **Matthew 17:20 (KJV)**

In this verse, Jesus points to what I call the nature of faith. Notice that faith is referred to as a mustard seed. Let's look at what it says in the NASB.

153

"And He said to them, "Because of the littleness of your faith; for truly I say to you, if you have faith the size of a mustard seed, you will say to this mountain, 'Move from here to there,' and it will move; and nothing will be impossible to you.'" **Matthew 17:20 (NASB)**

There are two phrases in this translation I want to focus upon: «**littleness of your faith**» and «**faith the size of a mustard seed.**» I don't necessarily like the phrase «**faith the size of a mustard seed**» because people take this exact wording and twist it to say what Jesus isn't saying. Have you heard someone say, "All you need is faith the size of a mustard seed?»

Do you know what you are encouraging? You are encouraging someone not to strengthen their faith, or their belief in God that moves them into partnership. When you say, «All you need is small faith,» you are hindering their miracle. If all I need is small faith, the faith the size of a mustard seed, then why would I go through the effort for it to increase? By doing so, when that mountain doesn't appear to be removed, some will lose all confidence in the workings of faith.

Jesus didn't say that your faith only needs to be the size of a mustard seed for you to move mountains. He said your faith needs to be as a mustard seed to move mountains. He was talking about the nature of faith-that faith operates like a seed. What does a seed do? -it grows! It moves from the smallest item to the tallest and most noticeable attraction. Yes, God has given each of us a measure of faith, but that doesn't' mean we can't increase the measure.

Look at the contradiction. First, Jesus instructed His disciples that they couldn't cast the demon out because of the «**littleness of their faith.**» Then He said that if faith is small like a mustard seed, they can move mountains. Does our normal interpretation make sense in that context? No! Instead, what Jesus is encouraging them to do is to strengthen and increase their faith-not to keep it small.

So, what does it mean to strengthen or increase your faith? Let's look at a tree. How do you know that a tree is strong? A tree isn't considered strong by its size, even though that often plays a factor. A tree is considered strong because of how much it can withstand-how much external pressure it can take and keep standing. A strong tree can withstand a hurricane. A strong tree can withstand a flood. A strong tree can withstand a blizzard. You have faith like that! No matter how strong the winds blow, no matter how long the winter lasts, when you are still standing in the grace of God and believing for your promise- you have faith and it's manifesting.

Let me put it simply. Strong faith lasts. Why? Because it's rooted in the Word of God. Look at what Jesus says in Matthew 7 about strength.

"Therefore, everyone who hears these words of Mine and acts on them, may be compared to a wise man who built his house on the rock. And the rain fell, and the floods came, and the winds blew and slammed against that house; and yet it did not fall, for it had been founded on the rock. Everyone who hears these words of Mine and does not act on them, will be like a foolish man who built his house on the sand. The rain fell, and the floods came, and the winds blew and slammed against that house; and it fell- and great was its fall."
Matthew 7:24-27 (NASB)

Notice the wording-those who hear His words and act on them. Does this sound familiar? This sounds like belief. Belief comes from hearing which moves you into action. What is it compared to? -a wise man who built his house on a rock. Now take this and add it to what Paul said about those who were left in the wilderness due to unbelief. **"And all drank the same spiritual drink, for they were drinking from a spiritual rock which followed them; and the rock was Christ."** (**1 Corinthians 10:4, NASB**). Why was the building able to withstand so much? -it was founded upon the rock that is Christ. Christ is your foundation, your beginning, and you will never fall if you build upon Him.

"And when Jesus entered Capernaum, a centurion came to Him, imploring Him, and saying, 'Lord, my servant is lying paralyzed at home, fearfully tormented.' Jesus said to him, 'I will come and heal him.' But the centurion said, 'Lord, I am not worthy for You to come under my roof, but just say the word, and my servant will be healed. For I also am a man under authority, with soldiers under me; and I say to this one, 'Go!' and he goes, and to another, 'Come!' and he comes, and to my slave, 'Do this!' and he does it." Now when Jesus heard this, He marveled and said to those who were following, 'Truly I say to you, I have not found such great faith with anyone in Israel.'" **Matthew 8:5-10 (NASB)**

What did Jesus consider to be great faith? Notice that the centurion didn't need to see the healing to believe that it was going to happen. Why? Because He believed that Jesus was a man of authority and all He had to do was speak. His faith was in the certainty of Christ's word. He said it, that settles it.

Think about it. We don't know how far away the centurion lived. It could have been a couple of minutes or hours‑ maybe more. As he went back home, the opportunity to step out of faith was available. He could have been thinking, "I do hope (wish) it worked." But we know that he was convinced that all Jesus had to do was speak, and it would be done. When Jesus said it, the centurion received it as a done deal, and no matter how long it took him to walk, he never moved from that stance. His faith lasted because he had a strong belief in Christ.

So, what is the nature of faith? Faith's nature is to grow. It starts off small, but as you grow your knowledge about Christ, it will deepen your belief, which in turn, will move you into action. Remember a seed eventually becomes a tree. It grows from being hidden to being seen. You can't see the seed when it's in the dirt, but as it grows it becomes more visible.

It's the same with your faith. In the beginning, it will be soft and personal. No matter how conservative and private it is, it's still faith. A lion doesn't need to be loud to be a lion. Faith doesn't need to be a huge spectacle to be faith. It isn't dependent on the size of your action, just that there is one. But as it grows through your knowledge and belief in Him, it will become more and more demonstrative. Where you gave $10 before, now you will give $100. Where you received healing for a headache before, now you will receive healing for cancer. Deepen your belief, grow your faith, and see God take you to new heights in Him and through Him.

Back in Matthew chapter 17, Jesus told the disciples that they didn't cast the demon out because their faith wasn't strong enough, their belief wasn't deep enough to partner with God on that level. But now notice what Jesus said following their questions, **"Howbeit this kind goeth not out but by prayer and fasting."** **(Matthew 17:21, NASB).** Now, remember, Jesus is teaching on New Covenant principles under the Old Covenant. Notice that He didn't say this kind leaves due to meditating on the Law. Focusing on self-effort wasn't going to help. He wanted them to pray and fast. In other words, He wanted them to talk to God and crucify their flesh.

We have already had a chapter on prayer, so this comes to no surprise to us. Prayer, through communication and revelation, makes us more like our God, enabling us to do what He does and think like He thinks. Because we're becoming more like Him through knowing Him, it's easier to respond when He speaks because it's familiar. Our partnership is strengthened, and it can withstand much, because we know Him.

Fasting is basically me saying "no" now, so I can say "yes" later. Through fasting, I'm telling my flesh "No." I'm making the choice to keep my flesh under my authority, which in turn will highlight God's voice, making it clearer. Fasting doesn't make God speak to you, it just makes His voice clearer because you have crucified the thing that was getting in the way. Because I hear better, I can partner better and easier.

So, let's look at all that we have covered in this chapter. We learned about the nature of faith. We have seen that faith was intended to grow and it grows through deepening your belief about Christ. As it grows, your demonstrations might be small and not obvious. That is okay because faith is supported by actions-not just big actions. But we know that as it grows, your small actions will become big actions making your faith more noticeable, not because you're forcing it, but because your belief has moved you into that level of partnership. Through prayer and fasting, we learned that our faith is strengthened and as a result, we have developed a strong partnership with God.

CONCLUSION

We covered a great amount of ground in this book. So, in closing I want to highlight a few things to get you started. This life of faith, this Process of Faith, this life of partnering with your God, hinges on what you believe. If you believe it, you will do it. If you believe that God loves you, then you will live like it's so. What you believe will echo through your life. If you don't like your life, change what you believe. How? -by changing what you have been saying and hearing. Speak God's truth, listen to God's truth, and see the truth. This will move you into partnership.

Start off small, it doesn't have to be big. God is patient. It's more important to Him for you to start than to be big about it. Don't worry, it will grow and with every new level of faith, your partnership with Him will increase, strengthening what you can receive and do.

I have poured out my heart and relayed what the Lord shared with me during this past season. The purpose of this book isn't to convince you. That's not my job. The purpose of this book is to give you something to think about-to offer an insight you might not have heard or thought through.

I will close with a similar question Jesus asked Martha.

"Jesus said to her, 'I am the resurrection and the life; he who believes in Me will live even if he dies, and everyone who lives and believes in Me will never die. Do you believe this?'" **John 11:25-26 (NASB)**

What do you believe? It doesn't matter what I believe, or what your parents believe, or what your pastor believes. They are not responsible for your partnership with your God. I believe this has been beneficial in one way or another to all who have read it. Receive from God, for He loves to give to you. Partner with God for He loves working with you. It's a process, not an equation.

Enjoy the journey with your God!!!

Biography

The Process of Faith is Nathaniel R. Horton's literary debut. Nathan grew up in a small town south of Dallas, TX. When he wasn't on the soccer fields, he could be found playing video games or simply hanging out with friends and family.

Although he grew up in church, Nathan's passion for the Word of God was not discovered until his early years of college.

Since then, he has spent most of his adult life cultivating that passion as a tool to help others clearly grasp Biblical truth.

www.ingramcontent.com/pod-product-compliance
Lightning Source LLC
Chambersburg PA
CBHW071220090426
42736CB00014B/2907